Help Yourself with Single-Session Therapy

Help Yourself with Single-Session Therapy provides an outlook on how you can help yourself with your emotional problems by using insights from single-session therapy.

Single-session therapy draws upon the skills and strengths of both the therapist and the client. The book will encourage you to develop your own solutions to your problems. Broken down into fourteen accessible chapters, it will help you to identify the problem before guiding you to provide your own goals and solutions. The importance of how to maintain change is also a key part of the process.

Help Yourself will be useful for all those who wish to help themselves with their emotional problems and for those who wish to support them. It will also be relevant for counsellors, psychotherapists and students in these disciplines who are interested in the application of very-brief therapy to self-help.

Windy Dryden, PhD, is Emeritus Professor of Psychotherapeutic Studies at Goldsmiths, University of London, and is an international authority on Rational Emotive Behaviour Therapy (REBT) and Single-Session Therapy (SST). He has worked in psychotherapy for over 45 years and is the author and editor of over 235 books.

Help Yourself with Single-Session Therapy

Windy Dryden

Routledge
Taylor & Francis Group

LONDON AND NEW YORK

First published 2021
by Routledge
2 Park Square, Milton Park, Abingdon, Oxon OX14 4RN

and by Routledge
52 Vanderbilt Avenue, New York, NY 10017

Routledge is an imprint of the Taylor & Francis Group, an informa business

British Library Cataloguing-in-Publication Data
A catalogue record for this book is available from the British Library

Library of Congress Cataloging-in-Publication Data
Names: Dryden, Windy, author.
Title: Help yourself with single-session therapy/
Windy Dryden, PhD.
Description: Abingdon, Oxon; New York, NY:
Routledge, 2021. | Includes index. |
Identifiers: LCCN 2020029599 (print) |
LCCN 2020029600 (ebook) | ISBN 9780367632632 (hardback) |
ISBN 9780367632625 (paperback) | ISBN 9781003114703 (ebook)
Subjects: LCSH: Single-session psychotherapy. |
Psychotherapist and patient.
Classification: LCC RC480.55 D75 2021 (print) |
LCC RC480.55 (ebook) | DDC 616.89/14–dc23
LC record available at https://lccn.loc.gov/2020029599
LC ebook record available at https://lccn.loc.gov/2020029600

ISBN: 978-0-367-63263-2 (hbk)
ISBN: 978-0-367-63262-5 (pbk)
ISBN: 978-1-003-11470-3 (ebk)

Typeset in Sabon
by Newgen Publishing UK

visit the eResources: www.routledge.com/9780367632625

While it is unlikely that you will only have one session of self-help therapy with yourself (although this could happen!), what this book will help you to do is to get down to the business of helping yourself quickly and get the most from every session that you have with yourself. During the book, I will introduce you to the power and potency of SST so that you can use the ideas that I will discuss in helping yourself deal with your own most pressing concern(s).

One of the things that I like about SST is that it encourages both the client and the therapist to bring to the session their respective skills and strengths. In this book then, I will encourage you to identify your own views about such issues as what factors are most involved in your problem, what you do that leads you to maintain the problem, albeit unwittingly, and what would be helpful elements of a good solution to your problem. In addition, I will offer you my perspective on these same issues, informed as this perspective is by the approach to therapy that I practise, i.e. REBT. Now you don't have to use these REBT insights, but they are there if you need them. Thus, you can rely on your own views, use those that stem from REBT or use what you consider to be the best from each. Whatever you decide to do is OK and does not change the fact that this book is largely based on insights derived from SST.

Windy Dryden, London & Eastbourne
June 2020

Preface

While I have written other self-help books, largely from the perspective of Rational Emotive Behaviour Therapy (REBT), a major approach within the tradition of Cognitive Behaviour Therapy, this present book is the first that I have written which shows you how you can help yourself by using insights derived from single-session therapy (SST). In SST the therapist and client meet with the expressed intention of helping the client in one session, knowing that more sessions are available if needed. I have been practising SST for a number of years now and I have been impressed with what can be achieved in one session when both therapist and client are prepared to work together in a focused way from moment one without the therapist spending time in usual therapeutic activities such as taking a case history, carrying out a full assessment or undertaking a case formulation before embarking on treatment.

What I have found particularly exciting about SST is that it encourages both therapist and client to make best use of the time that they have together and focus on the client's most pressing concern. The fallback position that more help is available if needed is akin to a safety net and the person who knows that help is available is comforted by this fact and may, as a result, not feel the need to use it.

Contents

Chapter 1

Why self-help?

Overview

In this chapter, I will consider the reasons why you might choose to help yourself with your psychological problem or problems, rather than seek help from another person. I discuss two types of reasons why you might choose self-help. The first is when you would prefer to be helped by another person, but for one or more reasons this is not possible. I call this 'self-help by default'. The second is when you prefer to help yourself rather than be helped by another person. I call this 'self-help by design'. However, I will begin the chapter by considering the three major settings in which you can be helped by another person if you live in Britain.

The contexts of being helped

If you have a psychological problem with which you have been grappling, there are several things you could do.

- You could decide to continue as you have been doing, struggling on, hoping that your problem will go away.
- You might speak to a non-professional about your problem. This will probably be someone you know, a trusted friend or family member perhaps.
- You could consult a trained professional (see below).

• You could embark on a programme of self-help which is the subject of this book.

Consulting a non-professional

If you decide to speak to a non-professional about your problem(s), and assuming that you have chosen somebody sympathetic, this person may respond in one of two ways. First, they may listen to you without interruption and give you the space to sort out the problem for yourself. I call this type of help 'listening-based help'. Second, they may listen to you and then give you advice based on their understanding of your problem and based on some ideas of what you can do to address the problem. I call this type of help 'listening plus advice-based help'. There is nothing wrong with either type of help and if you find what the other person has done helpful, then all well and good.

Consulting a professional

You may have spoken to one or more trusted people in your life, but not found the help they offered to you useful. As a result, you may want to consider consulting a trained mental health professional, such as a counsellor or a psychotherapist. There are three major ways of consulting such a helping professional in Britain.

Consulting a professional in the National Health Service

First, you may decide to see a trained professional who works in the National Health Service (NHS). After all, you have probably contributed to the upkeep of this service through paying taxes and making National Insurance (NI) contributions, and therefore you may feel entitled to get some help when you need it. Again, this is a perfectly valid route to seeking help for your problems, and you may wish to take it. If so, you can contact your GP who may offer you medication and/or refer you to one of the talking therapies provided by a service known as IAPT, which stands for

'Improving Access to the Psychological Therapies'. Increasingly, you can refer yourself directly to an IAPT service. You will be assessed and offered help based on that assessment of the nature of your problem(s). There will be a waiting list for that help depending upon how severe your problem is and the locality in which you live. However, there will be a limit to how much help you will be offered.

Consulting a professional in a charitable or non-profit organisation

Second, you may refer yourself to a counselling service run by a charitable or non-profit organisation. Once again, it is likely that you will be assessed and there will be a waiting list for help, again dependent upon an assessment of your need. While ongoing help may be offered in such a service, increasingly this is less likely now than it used to be. Why is this? In my view, one of the contributory factors, paradoxically, is that people in Britain are becoming more accepting of psychological problems in themselves and in others than was previously the case. We are increasingly being encouraged to see that it is not shameful to struggle emotionally and to come forward for help. As we are heeding this message, more and more of us are seeking help from trained mental health professionals, but unfortunately there are insufficient counsellors and therapists in place to offer help to those who are now seeking it. Consequently, NHS services and charitable, not-for-profit agencies are having to cap services, and even then waiting lists are growing.

Consulting a professional in private practice (going private)

The third way of accessing therapeutic services in Britain is by seeking a therapist or counsellor privately. If you take this route, you will either pay for counselling or therapy yourself or have it paid for you if you have private health insurance which covers you for such services. Private practitioners will tend not to put a cap on how much therapy they will offer you, and as such it is useful to agree a set number of sessions with the therapist at the outset to determine such issues as how you get on with the practitioner and how much progress you are making.

All help ultimately is self-help

Having outlined the contexts in which a person in Britain can seek therapeutic help, let me make a point which you may not have appreciated fully. It is this: *all help is ultimately self-help.*

I practise a form of therapy known as Rational Emotive Behaviour Therapy (REBT) and I will share insights from REBT as appropriate throughout the book. REBT is a therapeutic approach which is best placed within the tradition of psychotherapy known as Cognitive Behaviour Therapy (better known as CBT). I am sometimes asked if CBT is effective. My response is: 'Probably, yes, if you use it, but definitely no if you don't.'

When a drug company researches the efficacy of a drug, the only way it can know its effect is if it is sure that the people in the drug trial have taken the drug. In the same way, the only way to judge how effective CBT is if we know that the person has used it in their own life. Thus, if someone is referred for CBT and does not put it into practice in their life, then this is hardly a fair test of the efficacy of the therapy. This is why I say that, ultimately, all therapy is self-therapy.

Two forms of self-help

In the overview at the beginning of the chapter, I distinguished between self-help by default and self-help by design. Let me now discuss each type more fully.

Self-help by default

If you have decided to help yourself by default, you want to be helped by a mental health professional, but for one or more reasons such help is not available. Here is a list of such reasons:

- **You have to wait too long for the person to offer you help.** Here, you want to be helped by a mental health professional, and you seek help from such a person, but you are placed on a very long waiting list for such help and the estimated waiting time is too much for you. Consequently, you decide to help yourself instead, but you do so with reluctance.

- **Help from a mental health professional is not available.** It may be the case that you want to consult a therapist or counsellor for your problem(s), but one is not available where you live, and you cannot afford to go private. Again, in this case, somewhat reluctantly, you decide to help yourself.
- **You cannot afford the help that you want.** Another situation occurs sometimes where help from a mental health professional who works in the NHS or non-profit sector is available to you, but it is not the kind of help that you are seeking. Here, the desired help is only available in the private sector, and you cannot afford to access such help. Faced with the choice between seeking undesired help from a mental health professional and helping yourself, you, again with reluctance, decide to help yourself.
- **Practicalities.** You may prefer to be helped by another person, but practicalities may interfere with this. For example, your working hours may preclude you from having therapy sessions, and thus you choose to help yourself, again reluctantly.

You will have seen from the above that when you seek self-help by default, you do so with reservations. I will discuss how to deal with this situation presently.

Self-help by design

By self-help by design, I mean a situation where you choose to help yourself with your psychological problem(s) even though help from others, particularly mental health professionals, is available. There are several reasons why you may favour self-help.

- **Autonomy.** If you have an autonomous personality style, you prefer to rely on your self-helping resources rather than be helped by another person. You may decide to consult a therapist, but it will be with the expressed intention of taking what you learn from the therapist and then helping yourself with it.

- **Self-empowerment.** Helping yourself may give you a sense of empowerment which you may not experience if you seek help from a therapist.
- **Self-help better fits your schedule.** You may be the kind of person who prefers to structure your time so that you can do things when it suits you rather than another person. If so, self-help is for you because you can choose to help yourself at any time rather than fit into the schedule of a therapist or counsellor.

The above three factors represent positive reasons for self-help. What follows is a situation where you might decide to help yourself to avoid experiencing a problem if you consulted a mental help professional.

- **Shame.** You may need help, but you prefer to help yourself because you feel ashamed about seeking help from another person. In this case, the first thing you may want to address is your feelings of shame about such help-seeking. Once you have done this, you will be in a better position to choose whether to seek help from a therapist or from yourself. I will expand on this subject in the following chapter.

Whether you have chosen to help yourself by design or by default, you will get the most from self-help if you apply what I call the self-help mindset, which I discuss in Chapter 4.

David Muss's suggestions for self-help

Before closing, I will offer my extrapolations from suggestions for helping yourself made by David Muss (2012) in his excellent self-help book on dealing with post-trauma stress entitled *The Trauma*

Chapter 2

Do you need help?

Overview

In this chapter, I will help you to decide two things: whether or not you have a problem and whether or not you need help with this problem. In doing so, I will consider the relationship between emotional problems and help-seeking. In particular, I will show you how to deal with two major blocks to addressing your problems: shame and ambivalence. I will also distinguish between reading this book and using it and will stress that only the latter will help you to effect change.

If you do not think that you have a problem, there is no point in seeking help

Please note that the question of whether you have a problem and the question of whether you need help are different. If you have decided that you do not have a problem, then you will not seek help, at least for that problem. Imagine going to see a therapist, and in response to being asked what your problem is, you say that you do not have one. Now, it sometimes happens that other people think you have a problem, and you do not, and I will discuss this presently. However, a good rule of thumb here is: no problem, no help-seeking and, in the context of this book's focus, no self-help.

Trap.[1] Drawing upon Muss's views, my position is that self-help may be particularly useful for the following people:

- those who fear that going for therapy will jeopardise their jobs if others find out about it
- those who have had therapy and did not find it helpful
- those who can see the sense of helping themselves by 'nipping problems in the bud' before they become entrenched
- those who wish to help themselves without using drugs or without seeing a therapist.

If it is clear to you that you have a problem that you want to help yourself with, then you may wish to skip Chapter 2 and go to Chapter 3. However, if you are not sure about this, then in the following chapter I cover the question of whether you may need help or not and also how to respond when you are ambivalent about being helped, even when that help comes from yourself.

---

1 If you suffer from post-traumatic stress, you would do well to consult David Muss's book on the subject: Muss, D. (2012). *The Trauma Trap*. London: Doubleday.

Reading and using this book

Please note that I distinguish between *reading* this book and *using* it.

What does reading the book mean?

Reading the book means that you passively engage with it and do not necessarily apply any of its suggestions to your problem if you have one. The purpose of *reading* the book is to discover its contents so that you can ascertain whether or not they make sense to you and, assuming that they do make sense to you, to decide whether or not you wish to use it to address your problem.

What does using the book mean?

If you have decided that you have a problem with which you want help, then using this book means taking your problem, focusing on it and using the suggestions that I will make throughout the book to help yourself with this problem (which I will refer to in this book as your *nominated* problem). Using this book, then, means that you actively engage with the book and that you apply its suggestions to your nominated problem (if they make sense to you, of course). Please note, therefore, that reading the book without using it will *not* help you with your problem.

Read the book before using it

It follows that if you do have a problem (see below), I suggest that you read this book before deciding to use it. Remember that the purpose of reading this book before you use it is to decide two things. The first is to decide whether or not the book makes sense to you. If it does not make sense to you, then there is no point in using it. Second, if it does make sense to you, you then need to decide whether or not you might benefit from using it. Even if the book makes sense to you, if you do not think that using it will benefit you, then, again, there is no point in you using it. In this case, I suggest that you give the book to a friend who may wish to use it and gain benefit from it. If, having read the book, you decide that it does make sense to you and you think that you can benefit from using it, then go back to the beginning of the book and use it.

You can still read this book even if you do not have a problem

If you do not have a problem, you can certainly still *read* this book, and I encourage you to do so because you might like to know how you could help yourself, should you have an emotional problem in the future. But for now, you will not need to *use* this book as you do not have a problem at present.

Practical problems and emotional problems

It is important to differentiate between having a practical problem and having an emotional problem. If you have a *practical* problem, such as not having a job when you want one or finding it difficult to meet a partner, then you will want to find a practical-focused solution to this practical problem (e.g. widening your job search or asking friends if they can introduce you to people whom they know might be eligible partners for you). If you have an *emotional* problem such as anxiety, guilt or unconstructive anger, then these emotions will tend to interfere with your life in important ways. As such, you will want an emotional-focused solution to this emotional problem, one which helps you to change your feelings so that they don't interfere with your life.

Now you can have an emotional problem about your practical problem, or you can have a practical problem without having an emotional problem about this practical problem. This book can provide help to you whether you have a practical problem and/ or an emotional problem. However, you will need to use different types of solutions for different types of problems: practical-focused solutions for practical problems and emotional-focused solutions for emotional problems.

Do you have a problem?

In this section, I will discuss two situations: i) where you have a practical problem and ii) where you have an emotional problem.

Do you have a practical problem?

You can be said to have a practical problem when you have something in your life that you would rather not have (e.g. a noisy neighbour), or you don't have something in your life that you would rather have (e.g. an interesting job). This is best classed as a practical problem when you don't have an emotional problem about it. When this is the case, then you can fully focus on getting rid of what you don't want in your life (if you can) and on getting what you do want in your life (again if you can). If you have an emotional problem about your practical problem, the former will usually preoccupy you and interfere with your practical problem-solving. This is why if you have a practical problem and an emotional problem about the practical problem, psychologists will encourage you to deal with the emotional problem first before you tackle the practical problem. For example, if your practical problem is living next to a noisy neighbour and you are furious about this (emotional problem), then it is best to deal with your fury first before tackling the practical problem; otherwise there is a good chance that being in a furious state of mind and taking action when you are in this state of mind will generally make matters worse.

Do you have an emotional problem?

How can you tell if you have an emotional problem? In one sense, you have an emotional problem when you think you have one. However, if you look more carefully at this question, you will probably see that having an emotional problem means that one or more of the following apply.

1. You are experiencing **emotions** which are both painful to you *and* lead you to become stuck in one or more important

aspects of your life. Emotional pain on its own is not necessarily a sign that you have a problem. An emotional problem tends to be emotional pain *plus* stuckness.

2. You are engaging in **behaviours** that are self-defeating and lead you to become increasingly stuck. These behaviours are characterised by i) avoidance, where you do not take up opportunities to face up to and tackle the problem in question, or by ii) dealing with the problem but in a way which leads to its continuation or worsening rather than its resolution.

3. You have **thoughts** and hold **attitudes** that both underpin your self-defeating emotions and unconstructive behaviours, as discussed above, and interfere with emotional problem-solving and, if relevant, practical problem-solving.

4. Your emotional problem is being masked by avoidance. This means that you take steps that prevent you from experiencing the full force of your emotional problem, but in doing so you are both restricting yourself and preventing yourself from dealing with your emotional problem.

In this book, I will focus largely on emotional problems, although you can also use the points that I will introduce and discuss to help yourself with your practical problem(s).

When others think you have a problem

If someone thinks that you have a problem (particularly an emotional problem) and brings this to your attention, then this could be the stimulus for you to consider whether or not they are correct. If you are open to considering this, then I suggest that you use the emotions/behaviour/thoughts–attitudes schema introduced above to help you make a decision on this point.

On the other hand, you may dismiss the other person's viewpoint out of hand. If you do so, it may be because you do not have an emotional problem, in which case there is no need to help yourself. However, you may dismiss the other person's view because you would feel ashamed if you did acknowledge that you have a problem. As such, this feeling of shame motivates you to deny the existence of the problem.

Dealing with feelings of shame

One of the paradoxes of self-help is that for you to deal with shame you need to acknowledge that this is a problem for you and the very thing that might stop you from doing this is your feeling of shame about feeling shame! One of the ways of dealing with this paradox is to assume that you do experience shame (whether you do or not) and to understand how to address it effectively.

One of the insights that comes from the field of single-session therapy (on which this book is based) is that it is often important for you to draw upon your successful experiences in dealing with the very problem on which you are focused. Thus, have you ever had the experience of feeling ashamed about something and addressing these feelings successfully? If so, did you do this by yourself or were others helpful to you? If you did this by yourself, what did you do or think that was helpful to you? If others were helpful to you, what did they do that was helpful to you? Use these factors in addressing your feelings of shame now.

One of the useful features of SST is that it encourages clients to identify their strengths as a person and then to apply these to address their problems, where appropriate. If clients are going to be encouraged to do this, then therapists should at least offer their clients the opportunity to hear their perspective on the clients' problems. Such expertise should be offered without the therapist becoming the 'expert' as a result.

My perspective on dealing with shame

In this section, I will first outline the factors involved in shame before arguing that 'disappointment' is the healthy alternative to shame.

What is shame?

In my view, shame, in this context, is the emotion you experience when i) you fall very short of your ideal or consider that you have revealed a weakness to yourself and/or to others, ii) you demand that you *must* not fall that short or have the weakness, and iii) you devalue yourself for falling very short of your ideal or having the weakness (e.g. 'I am defective' or 'I am a weak, pathetic person').

Disappointment: the healthy alternative to shame

The healthy alternative to shame, in my view, is disappointment. This is the emotion you experience when i) you again fall very short of your ideal or consider that you have revealed a weakness to yourself or to others, ii) you acknowledge that you would prefer not to fall that short or have the weakness, and iii) you accept yourself as an ordinary, fallible human being for falling very short of your ideal or having the weakness (e.g. 'I am fallible' or 'I am not a weak, pathetic person; I am acceptable as a person to myself whether or not I fall very short of my ideal or have the weakness').

You will notice that the inferences that you have fallen very short of your ideal and that you have revealed a weakness to yourself and/ or to others are common to both shame and disappointment. The best time to examine such inferences is when you are in the right frame of mind to do so, which in this case is when you are experiencing shame-free disappointment rather than shame.

Work to change your attitude

As should be clear from the above, in my view the best way to address your shameful feelings which lead you to deny that you have a problem is by changing the attitudes that underpin shame to the attitudes that underpin disappointment. Basically, you have a choice of two attitudes as shown in Table 2.1.

Once you have chosen to operate according to attitudes of flexibility and unconditional self-acceptance,[1] then underpin this choice with arguments that support these attitudes. One way of doing so is to imagine that if someone you care for has fallen very short of their ideal or revealed a weakness to themself and/or to

---

1 Hopefully, you have chosen the attitudes of flexibility and unconditional self-acceptance. If you genuinely want to operate on the attitudes of rigidity and self-devaluation, then you need to discuss this with a therapist.

Table 2.1 Attitudes that underpin shame (rigid and self-devaluaxtion) and disappointment (flexible and unconditional self-acceptance)

Rigid Attitude	Flexible Attitude
'I must not fall very short of my ideal or have the weakness'	'I would prefer not to fall very short of my ideal or have the weakness, but sadly my preferences do not have to be met'

Attitude of Self-Devaluation	Attitude of Unconditional Self-Acceptance
'I am a weak, pathetic person for falling very short of my ideal or having the weakness'	'I am not a weak, pathetic person; I am acceptable as a person to myself whether or not I fall very short of my ideal or have the weakness'

others, which of the above attitude pairs would you encourage them to adopt and why? Then, apply these same arguments if you need to when rehearsing the attitudes of flexibility and unconditional self-acceptance.

As a result of this work, you should now be in a position to admit to yourself that you have a problem.

When you decide not to seek help for your problem

If you have decided that you do have a problem, the next step is to decide whether or not you want help with this problem. One of my acquaintances is fearful of riding on the London Underground. She recognises that she has a problem, but she does not want to seek help for it. Why? While she acknowledges that her anxiety has costs (it takes her much longer to get around London), she has found a way around her problem (she takes buses or taxis instead). The costs of having the problem are, in her mind, lower than the perceived costs of being helped or helping herself with it.

The takeaway from this vignette is that just because you have a problem, it does not follow that you will seek help for it.

Are you ambivalent about seeking help for your problem?

You may have a problem and be ambivalent about seeking help for it, even from yourself.[2] In this context, ambivalence means that you have reasons for seeking help for your problem and reasons not to.

Deal with ambivalence

If you are ambivalent about seeking help, then here is one way of dealing with it.

Step 1: Accept that you are ambivalent

If the reality is that you are ambivalent, then you have two main choices: to accept this reality or to reject it. If you reject your ambivalence, the chances are that you are demanding that you must not be ambivalent. In this case, please recognise that while you might prefer not to be ambivalent, the fact is that you are, and you don't have to be ambivalent free. Acceptance here means acknowledging the reality of a situation even though you may not like it. If you accept the reality of your ambivalence, then you will be much more likely to address it than if you reject that reality.

Step 2: List your reasons to help yourself with your problem

The next step is for you to explore your ambivalence. Start by listing the reasons in favour of you helping yourself with your problem. I suggest that you do this in writing. Table 2.2 presents such a form.

---

2 From this point on, when I write about seeking help, I mean seeking help from yourself, better known as self-help.

Table 2.2 **Dealing with your ambivalence about helping yourself with your problem**

State Your Problem:

List Your Reasons to Help Yourself with Your Problem:

1.

2.

3.

4.

5.

6.

7.

8.

9.

10.

List Your Reasons Not to Help Yourself with Your Problem	Respond to These Reasons
1.	1.
2.	2.
3.	3.
4.	4.
5.	5.
6.	6.
7.	7.
8.	8.
9.	9.
10.	10.

Decision: Based on the above, I have decided to/not to* help myself with my problem.

* Delete as appropriate.

The reasons might include:

- I want to get unstuck and move on and thus be better able to achieve my goals.
- I want to change unhealthy patterns of thinking, feeling and behaviour especially concerning the adversity that features in my problem.
- I want to be better able to face up to the adversity and to change it if I can change it or to tolerate it better if I can't change it.
- I want to get along better with other people.
- I want to feel more comfortable in my own skin.
- I want to live a life more attuned with my values.

Step 3: List your reasons not to help yourself with your problem

Then, list the reasons not to help yourself with the problem. Do so in the left-hand column of the *second* section of Table 2.2. These might include:

- I will feel more uncomfortable in the short term if I face up to what I have been avoiding.
- I will lose the sense of familiarity that my problem gives me and instead I will experience uncertainty.
- I will have to move away from friends or relatives and other people who support my problem.
- I will lose the material advantages that my problem gives me.
- Helping myself with my problem will be 'too' hard.
- I won't know what will happen if I do decide to help myself.
- I don't feel confident about helping myself.

Step 4: Stand back, and from a distance look at your reasons not to help yourself and respond to them

After you have listed reasons not to help yourself with your problem, take a break, stand back, consider these reasons and respond to them using the right-hand column of the second section of Table 2.2. Table 2.3 lists possible responses to the reasons for not helping yourself with your problem listed above.

List Your Reasons Not to Help Yourself with Your Problem	Respond to These Reasons
1. I will feel more uncomfortable in the short term if I face up to what I have been avoiding.	1. Yes, it's true that I will feel more uncomfortable if I face what I have been avoiding, but that discomfort is worth putting up with if it means that I will deal with my problem and the discomfort will probably be time limited.
2. I will lose the sense of familiarity that my problem gives me and instead I will experience uncertainty.	2. Yes, doing something to help myself with my problem will probably feel strange and unfamiliar and things may be uncertain for a while. However, these states will probably be time limited and it is worth it to me to tolerate them if it means that I deal with my problem.
3. I will have to move away from friends or relatives and other people who support my problem.	3. If that is the case, then I am going to have to prioritise my mental well-being over these relationships, sad though this may be. If I don't look after myself, who will?
4. I will lose the material advantages that my problem gives me.	4. Again if this is the case, addressing my problem effectively is more important to me in the longer term than these material advantages.
5. Helping myself will be 'too' hard.	5. Helping myself may be hard, but too hard? Certainly not!
6. I won't know what will happen if I do embark on helping myself.	6. This is true, but if I tolerate not knowing and focus on addressing my problem, then I will find out soon enough. When I do find out, I will deal with whatever comes up.
7. I don't feel confident about helping myself.	7. Confidence comes from doing things unconfidently. So not feeling confident about helping myself is not a barrier to self-help unless I let it be a barrier.

Step 5: Decide whether or not to help yourself with your problem

Having specified reasons in favour of helping yourself and responded to listed reasons for not doing so, you should be in a position to make up your mind about whether or not to embark on the process of self-help. I will now assume that you have decided to do so.

Naomi

Throughout this book, I will refer to the experiences of a person whom I call Naomi whose problem is in the realm of work. She became depressed every time her work was criticised. Even when her boss praised her work, his well-meaning suggestion about how she could do even better resulted in virulent self-criticism. While Naomi always handed in her work on time, she would spend a great deal of her spare time on work projects so that she would not be criticised. Her goal was to deal with criticism in a healthier way and to spend her spare time on non-work activities. While she wanted to spend non-work time with her friends, she was ambivalent about doing so because she feared that the quality and thoroughness of her work might suffer both in her mind and in the minds of others. On weighing up the pros and cons of helping herself on this issue, Naomi considered that if she continued to spend her spare time on work, then her friendships would suffer and she would eventually burn out, and this would affect the quality of her work.

In the following chapter, I will focus on single-session therapy on which this book is based and will outline its major principles. In doing so, I will focus on how SST can be useful as a framework for self-help.

Chapter 3

What is single-session therapy (SST)?

Overview

In this chapter, I will focus on the nature of single-session therapy. After briefly discussing its origins, I distinguish between SST that lasts for one session with no prospect of further help and SST where the therapist and client embark on the process with the intention of helping the client in one session but where they agree that further sessions are available if needed. While both may be referred to as single-session therapy, some people prefer calling the latter 'One-at-a-Time Therapy'. I note that it is most likely that you will have more than one session of self-help and as such, so that you get the most out of the first and any subsequent sessions you have with yourself, I suggest that you engage in a process known as 'reflect–digest–act–wait–decide'.

The origins of SST

Some attribute the birth of SST to Sigmund Freud, who at the end of the nineteenth century and the beginning of the twentieth century saw two people for a single session while on vacation and did so as a favour to them. Given the circumstances, Freud tailored his therapeutic interventions according to the time that he had at his disposal. But perhaps the origins of modern-day SST can be traced to Moshe Talmon, an Israeli psychologist, who in

1990 wrote a book entitled *Single Session Therapy: Maximising the Effect of the First (and Often Only) Therapeutic Encounter.* This book was based on the experiences of Talmon who spent some time at the Kaiser Permanente Medical Centre in California in the mid-1980s. During the early part of his work at the clinic, Talmon found that a sizeable number of his family clients (200) did not return for a second session despite being offered one (i.e. their single session was often unplanned). Rather than accept the usual reasons for such a frequently occurring phenomenon (e.g. 'They are drop-outs; these things happen' or 'They weren't ready to change'), Talmon took an unprecedented step. He contacted the 200 cases he had seen for one session to find out from them what accounted for their single clinic attendance. To his surprise, he found that '78 percent of the 200 patients I called said that they had got what they wanted out of the single session and felt better or much better about the problem that had led them to seek therapy' (Talmon, 1990: 9).[1] Since then, counsellors and therapists throughout the world have become interested in SST and between 2012 and 2019 three international symposia on SST have been held, two in Australia and one in Canada. There are plans to hold the fourth international symposium in Italy in 2024.

What is SST?

In one sense, it is clear what SST is:

Single-session therapy is a single session of therapy, normally provided by a therapist who collaborates with a client with the intention of helping that client to achieve at the end of the session whatever that person came to the session to achieve.

However, as with many things in life, the reality is often more complex than this. Thus, I will take the above statement and

---

1 Talmon. M. (1990). *Single Session Therapy: Maximizing the Effect of the First (and Often Only) Therapeutic Encounter.* San Francisco, CA: Jossey-Bass.

consider it more closely, especially as the issues it raises pertain to self-help.

Is SST really a single session of therapy?

The answer to this question is 'yes' and 'no'. When the answer to the question is 'yes', the therapist and client agree beforehand that, for whatever reason, they will meet for one session and one session only. For example, I do a number of training workshops on single-session therapy, and in the course of a workshop I will do one or two demonstrations of the way I practise SST. Beforehand, I make it very clear to potential volunteer clients that the session we will have will be the only one I will have with them, and they volunteer on that basis.

When the answer to the above question is 'no', the therapist and client set out with the intention of only meeting once, but they both agree, at the outset, that further help is available, if needed. This might be another single session, or it may involve the client seeking a different form of help based on an assessment of the client's needs made jointly by the client and the therapist.

One-at-a-Time Therapy

When it is clear, at the outset, that clients may have access to further help if needed, some therapists prefer to use the term 'One-at-a-Time Therapy' (OAATT) rather than the term 'Single-Session Therapy' (SST). OAATT can be defined as follows:

> One-at-a-Time Therapy again involves a single session of therapy, normally provided by a therapist who collaborates with a client with the intention of helping that client as much as possible in that session, with both knowing that further help is available should it be needed. Therapy proceeds one session at a time until the client has achieved what they set out to achieve. Blocks of sessions are incompatible with OAATT since these involve several sessions contracted for in advance.

You will see from this definition that OAATT overlaps signifi-
cantly with the definition of SST where further help is available
and, for the purposes of this book, the terms can be considered
interchangeable since when it comes to self-help, it is unlikely that
you will only need one session with yourself to help yourself.

What is a session?

Traditionally, in counselling and psychotherapy, a 'session' is usually a 'therapeutic hour' which lasts for 50 minutes. This enables
the counsellor to devote time between sessions to writing notes
and to personal care activities. In SST, sessions can be shorter
or longer than 50 minutes depending upon such matters as the
person's problem and how many clients are in the room with the
therapist.

When it comes to self-help, the concept of a 'session' is quite
novel. I define a session of self-help as an extended period of time
which you devote to helping yourself with a nominated problem
or issue. How long such a session will last will also vary and will
depend upon such matters as the nature of your problem, how
much time you have to devote to self-help on any one occasion
and how quickly you can work on your issue. I encourage you to
work on your nominated problem(s) at your own speed and not
to concern yourself with such matters as how long a session of
self-help should ideally last.

Reflect–digest–act–wait–decide

Given that you will probably need more than one self-help
session, here are some suggestions to help you to get the best out
of every session that you have with yourself. After you have had
a self-help session, engage with a five-step process that I refer to
here as 'reflect–digest–act–wait–decide' (see Chapter 6). Basically,
this means that you reflect on what you have learned from a self-
help session, digest the learning, act on the digested learning and
wait for a while to see the impact of what you have done before
deciding what to do next.

Using this five-stage process, you can help yourself session by session until you have solved your nominated problem and any related problems.

Why single-session therapy?

You may still be wondering why SST exists? After all, it does sound counterintuitive since you might expect that the first session in psychotherapy or counselling would be devoted to an assessment of the client and their concerns before the therapist recommends a particular course of 'treatment'. Of course, this does happen. However, there are some surprising findings which cast doubt about the value of this 'assessment before therapy' approach in all cases,

The first surprising finding is that in both public therapy agencies and in non-governmental therapy agencies, such as those run by charities,[2] the most frequent number of sessions that clients have is '1' followed by '2' followed by '3' (Hoyt & Talmon, 2014).[3] When therapists learn of this finding, they tend to conclude that this is proof that clients are generally dissatisfied with the therapy that they have received and can be said to have 'dropped out' of treatment. However, the second surprising research finding is that 70%—80% of clients who attended a single session were satisfied with that session and did not seek further help (Hoyt & Talmon, 2014).

Given that clients can be helped quickly and are generally satisfied with such help, it is useful to ask what they find helpful about SST and how these helpful ingredients can be used by you when you come to help yourself with your problem(s). This book is devoted to answering this question.

---

2 We do not know what the comparable figure is in private practice settings because private practitioners are not asked to provide such data.
3 Hoyt, M.F., & Talmon, M.F. (2014). What the literature says: An annotated bibliography. In M.F. Hoyt & M. Talmon (Eds.), *Capturing the Moment: Single Session Therapy and Walk-In Services* (pp. 487–516). Bethel, CT: Crown House Publishing.

Having considered the nature of single-session therapy in this chapter, in the next chapter I will discuss what I call the 'single-session self-help mindset'. The more you have the elements of this mindset and are prepared to act on them, the more successful your self-help efforts will be.

Chapter 4

Use the single-session self-help mindset

Overview

When I train therapists in single-session therapy, I outline a particular single-session mindset that such therapists need to adopt if they are going to work effectively in SST. In doing so, I note that clients also need to adopt their own single-session mindset if they are going to benefit from SST. In this chapter, I will consider and discuss elements of this latter mindset and show you how you can apply these elements to self-help to encourage you to get the most out of your self-helping efforts based on SST. I call this the single-session self-help mindset.

Use elements of the single-session self-help mindset

The more of the following elements you can use while helping yourself, the more effective your self-help efforts are likely to be. In this chapter, I will briefly review these self-helping elements and elaborate on them in the rest of the book.

Take away something meaningful from each session of self-help

However many sessions you have with yourself as you address your problem(s), it would be useful for you to use one of the guiding principles of single-session therapy as you do so. This is: take away something meaningful from each session of self-help. This ideally should be something significant that is related to the problem that you are addressing and to its possible solution.

Use the growth mindset

Carol Dweck (2017) distinguishes between what she calls a 'growth mindset' and a 'fixed mindset'.[1] The former argues that intelligence can be developed rather than being static as in the latter. The growth mindset has the following features.

Embrace challenges rather than avoid them

As you do so, I recommend that you use a principle that I refer to as 'challenging, but not overwhelming'. This means that as you face your adversities, do so in a way that is challenging for you, but which you do not regard as overwhelming at the time.

Persist in the face of setbacks rather than give up

You will likely experience setbacks as you implement your self-help programme. You can view a setback as providing valuable information about what you need to change in this programme. Or you could see it as a sign that you will never reach your goal and thus give up. Persistence will help you do the former rather than the latter.

Effort is the necessary path to problem-solution

While it would be nice to solve your problems effortlessly, this is unrealistic. Seeing effort as necessary in the change process

1 Dweck, C (2017). *Mindset: Changing the Way You Think to Fulfil Your Potential*. London: Robinson.

and implementing this view will help you solve your nominated problem(s).

Learn from others

Others can be the source of learning how to solve your problem(s). Thus, you can learn from how others have solved similar problems, and you can learn from others' suggestions about how you can address your problem. Having said this, only use solutions that make sense to and work for you.

Use the power of now

The principle of the 'power of now' states that although you may set goals in the future and be influenced by what has gone on in the past, you live in the 'now' and as such you can only help yourself 'in the now'. So, stop thinking that you are a prisoner of the past and stop putting off helping yourself to some unspecified time in the future when the time is 'right' for you to do so and help yourself 'now'.

Identify your strengths and utilise them in the session

Single-session therapists encourage their clients to utilise their strengths as a person to help them get the most out of their therapy sessions. The reason is that in SST there is not sufficient time to help clients develop skills that are not currently in their repertoire. In self-help, since you are not working with a therapist who could teach you new relevant skills, *you* should identify the strengths that you have as a person and use these in selecting and implementing the most viable solution to your nominated problem(s).

Identify potentially helpful resources in the environment and make use of them as you address your problem

Single-session therapists also encourage their clients to identify external resources in their environment that they can use to help solve their problem. This is a strategy that you could implement in your self-help endeavours. One such external resource is people known to you who might help or encourage you as you set about addressing your nominated problem(s).

Focus on one issue or problem

In 2006, Boots, the health and beauty retailer and pharmacy chain in the United Kingdom, ran a campaign for people wishing to keep to their New Year's resolutions which they called 'Change One Thing'. They argued, correctly in my view, that if you try to change one problematic thing, you will tend to be more successful than if you try to change several problems at once. So, unless you have a good reason to do otherwise, identify one issue or problem and focus on this until you have achieved your goal. Then, if relevant, choose another problem and work on that.

Take appropriate responsibility

In my view, you are responsible for what you can control. So, when you are thinking about the problem that you wish to address, work out what you can and what you can't control. A good rule of thumb is this: your thinking, your feelings, your behaviour and your decisions are within your control and therefore you are responsible for them. The ways other people think, feel and behave are outside your control, and therefore you are not responsible for them. Having said that, you can influence other people, but you can only do so through your own behaviour, as will be discussed in the following section.

The important point about the responsibility principle is that it helps you to appreciate that while your environment, both past and present, may influence you, it does not constrain you, and that you can transcend situations by choosing how to respond to them.

Assess your problem and change what you can control, not what you can't

Following on from the above point, when you set about addressing your problem, it is important that you target for change relevant problem-related factors that you can control. As outlined above, this means changing some aspect of your thinking or your behaviour. It also means that you can attempt to influence the situation you are in, including the behaviour of others, but you can only do so by changing some aspect of your own behaviour. So if you are in a problematic relationship with another person, for example, and you want to change this relationship, you can only do so by changing what you can control in this situation. Thus, you can change the way you think about the other person and, more importantly, you can change the way you act towards the other person. When you make such changes, see the impact that they have on the other. You may have to experiment with different ways of relating to the other before you see a change in them. If no change is forthcoming, you still have a choice: you can choose to remain in the relationship, or you can choose to leave the relationship. If you do the former, then you need to develop an attitude that enables you to remain in the relationship as healthily as possible.

Set a goal for each self-help session

There are two types of goals that you need to be concerned with as you address your problem(s). The first relates to the problem that you have nominated for attention. Here it is useful to have a realistic picture of what would be different so that you would regard the problem as solved. The second is concerned with every session that you have with yourself. Here a good question to ask yourself is: 'What would I *realistically* like to achieve from this session that will make me pleased that I had it?' Please note the emphasis that I placed on the word 'realistically' here. By all means, stretch yourself in the session goal you set, but do not make it so unrealistic that you end up by being discouraged because you have failed to achieve it.

Focus on available solutions and select the most viable

Once you have understood the problem and are clear what you need to change, then you need to list the possible solutions to your problem and select the one that is the most viable. This is the solution that you think you can implement rather than the most effective one, for you may conclude that you may not be able to put the latter into effect.

Rehearse the solution in your self-help session

You would probably not buy a car before test driving it first, would you? In the same vein, you need to rehearse your selected solution before deciding whether or not to implement it in your life. Such rehearsal may take place in your mind's eye, or you may wish to rehearse it with a person you have asked to help you as you address your problem. The main purpose of this rehearsal is to help you gain some experience in using the solution in order to see if it suits you. You may like the look of a car in a showroom but decide that it is not for you once you have driven it. If you decide, based on such rehearsal, not to implement your selected solution, you will have saved yourself time but will then need to review the remaining solutions and choose the one that again seems most viable. Even if you have decided to implement the rehearsed solution, such rehearsal may lead you to 'tweak' the solution in certain ways to increase the chances of implementing it in real-life situations.

Implement your selected solution and evaluate its effects

Once you have selected a solution and rehearsed it, the next step is for you to implement it where it matters, in a real-life situation where your adversity is actually present or may well be present. For example, if your nominated problem is anxiety about failing an important task, then you need to implement your selected solution in a situation where the prospect of failure exists. After you have implemented the solution, you need to evaluate its effects. In this respect, it is useful to think of both the immediate and longer-term effects of your implemented solution. In Chapter 3, I introduced the 'reflect–digest–act–wait–decide' process, which I will discuss more fully in Chapter 6. In this regard, once you take 'action', you 'wait' for the consequences of your actions to become clear and then you 'decide' what to do as a result. If, after a while, your implemented solutions have proven to be ineffective, then you need to reassess the situation as you may have missed an important ingredient which you need to take into account in developing a different, more effective solution.

Identify and deal with obstacles to change

The process of change is rarely smooth and, as such, you need to deal with any obstacles to change you may encounter. The best way to deal with obstacles to change is to anticipate the relevant factors and deal with them before these factors become obstacles. I will deal with the issue more fully in Chapter 13.

Maintain your gains

Once you have achieved your goal and have dealt successfully with your problem(s), then you will need to take steps to maintain your gains. Otherwise, you may slip back to the old ways of thinking and behaving that were implicated in your problem (see Chapter 14).

Generalise your learning

Once your implemented solutions have proven to be effective with your nominated problem(s), and you have maintained these gains, then you can think of generalising these solutions to other related problems you may have, if relevant (see Chapter 14).

In this chapter, I have reviewed the elements of what I call the single-session self-help mindset, which are the foundations of effective self-help based on the insights from single-session therapy. In the coming chapters, I will discuss how to implement this mindset, beginning with what you need to do to prepare yourself for change.

Chapter 5

Prepare yourself for change

Overview

At the outset, I will assume that you have made a decision to address a problem you currently have and that this problem is an emotional one.[1] I will also assume that you have dealt with your ambivalence and/or your feelings of shame about addressing this problem. However, if you are still ambivalent or ashamed about addressing your nominated problem(s), read and use the relevant sections in Chapter 2 (see pp. 13–21).

In this chapter, I will discuss what you can do to prepare yourself to address your nominated problem(s). These preparations, which are again derived from the practice of single-session therapy, are foundational in that they underpin whatever you decide to do to tackle your problem(s). Thus, you can prepare for embarking on a self-help programme by selecting one problem to work on at a time and being clear with yourself why you want to address your nominated problem. You can save time by understanding your previous attempts to help yourself with the problem and being clear with yourself regarding what was helpful and what was not helpful about these problem-solving attempts. Setting goals is also important, as is getting yourself into a general problem-solving state

---

1 Although, as I discussed in Chapter 2, you can also use the material in this book to help you with your practical problem(s).

of mind. I then encourage you to identify your internal strengths and external resources since drawing upon both sets of factors can be very useful to you throughout the self-help process. Finally, I make the point that no matter how many sessions of self-help you have, preparing for every session can help you substantially.

Problem selection

Before you set off on a programme of self-help, be clear with yourself about what is the one problem you wish to focus on right now. You may have several problems, but it is best to deal with them one at a time, and you stand the best chance of success if you select the problem that is most important to *you* to address. In this book, I call this problem the *nominated problem*.

Determine the effects of your nominated problem

Before you embark on a self-help programme, be clear why your problem is a problem for you. You can best do this by asking yourself questions about the effects of your problem. I suggest that you think about the effects of your problem on you and on relevant other people in your life. Do this from both a short-term perspective and a long-term perspective. List relevant effects and use Table 5.1 to keep a written record of them. Here are some questions that you might find useful in this respect.

• Does my problem affect my work and, if so, how?
• Does my problem affect my relationships and, if so, how?
• Does my problem result in me avoiding any situations that it would be important for me not to avoid?
• Does my problem adversely affect significant others in my life and, if so, how?

Reasons for addressing the problem

By now it should be clear that your nominated problem really is a problem for you.

Table 5.1 The short-term and long-term consequences of having your problem for yourself and for relevant others

	Short-Term Consequences	Long-Term Consequences
Consequences for Self		
Consequences for Relevant Others		

However, just because it is a problem for you, it does not follow that you will wish to change it or are willing to commit to taking the steps required to change it. So, the next step is for you to state the reasons why you want to change the problem and the reasons why you are prepared to take steps to find and implement a solution to the problem. Being clear about both sets of reasons will serve as good foundations for self-help. So often people begin to address their problems without having the clarity that I am suggesting that you should have concerning the reasons for addressing your nominated problem.

Understand previous attempts to solve the problem

Another important thing that you can do to prepare for helping yourself with your nominated problem is to list the things you have done in the past to address your problem. Ask yourself the following questions:

- **What have I tried in the past that has helped with this problem?**
  Identify the factors that were helpful to you and make a note of them so that you can make use of them when you later devise a solution to your nominated problem.
- **What have I tried that has not helped with the problem or made it worse?**
  Identify the factors that were not helpful (or were indeed unhelpful) to you and make a note of them so that you can refrain from using them when you later devise the aforementioned solution. Many people keep on using strategies to help themselves deal with their problems that have not proven helpful. This is a trap that it is important for you to avoid.

Set goals for self-help

It is important that you are clear with yourself about what you want to achieve from the process of self-help. There are two occasions where you will need to set goals. The first is here when you are preparing to embark on the self-help process. The second occurs after you have a clearer understanding of your nominated problem (see Chapter 8).

Setting a goal for your nominated problem before you begin the self-help process involves you having a clear idea of how you could handle situations in which you have the problem differently. A good rule of thumb is if you can't see it, it is not a good goal. When asked what they want to achieve concerning their problem, many people indicate the absence of their problem as their problem-related goal. For example:

> Problem: I am anxious about talking in front of a group.
> Problem-related goal: I don't want to be anxious about talking in front of a group.

It is difficult to see yourself *not* being anxious, so this is not a good goal.

Compare the following:

> Problem: I am anxious about talking in front of a group.
> Problem-related goal: I want to be concerned about talking in front of a group, but not anxious.

By contrast, it is possible to see yourself being concerned, but not anxious. This involves the presence of the desired state (concerned), which is contrasted with the problematic state. Consequently, this is a good goal.

Access a problem-solving mindset

One particularly useful way of preparing yourself to help yourself is to access a problem-solving mindset. Doing so will help you to develop realistic expectations of dealing effectively with your nominated problem(s). You can do this as follows: 'Remember a problem that happened any time in your life that you resolved in such a way that left you feeling proud of yourself. What did you do that left you feeling proud of yourself?'

Access this problem-solving mindset and use it as you address your nominated problem.

Identify internal strengths

One of the best ways that you can prepare yourself for self-help is to identify internal strengths that you have as a person which you can bring to the process that will help you to address your nominated problem(s) and achieve your goal(s). Here are some examples of strengths to stimulate your thinking on this point, if needed:

- love
- humour
- kindness
- social intelligence
- open-mindedness
- compassion
- leadership
- perseverance
- wisdom
- resilience
- spirituality
- self-control.

If you are struggling to identify your strengths, the following questions may help you:[2]

1. What would people who know you very well say if asked what your strengths are?
2. If you went for an interview for a job that you really wanted and they asked you to name your strengths, what would you say?

If you have more than one problem that you want to tackle, then it may be that different problems require different strengths. Please bear this in mind as you go forward.

---

2 You can take a free survey to identify your character strengths at www. viacharacter.org.

Identify external resources

External resources are people, organisations and objects in your environment that may be helpful to you as you address your nominated problems. When it comes to people in your environment, then the following commonly used question may be particularly helpful to you: 'Who in your life right now could help you as you address the problem?' While it is true that only you can help yourself, it is also true that you do not have to do this alone. Some people resonate to the concept of 'team', as in 'Who is on your team that can provide help to you as you address your problem?' It is probably the case that different people on your team may provide different kinds of help to you. For example, one 'team member' might help you brainstorm and evaluate different solutions to your problem, while another may show tender loving care (TLC) when things are going wrong for you. Knowing who is on your team and what help they can give you is important, so make a list and keep this to hand as you embark on your self-help programme (see Table 5.2).

Prepare for each self-help session

In my therapy practice, I have noticed that unless I encourage them to do so, my clients do not generally prepare for their therapy sessions. A major insight from SST is that it is important for people seeking help to use time effectively both in therapy sessions and before (and after) therapy sessions. This is true in self-help therapy too. Prepare for each session of self-help by asking yourself what you want to achieve from the session. Make this as realistic as possible. Doing this will help you to focus on what you want to achieve from the session and avoid getting distracted with other factors that may not be relevant to emotional problem-solving.

Your session preparation will be guided by where you are in the process concerning dealing with your nominated problem.

In the next chapter, I will discuss a process that I call the 'reflect–digest–act–wait–decide' process. Implementing this process will help you get the most out of every session of self-help that you have.

Table 5.2 **Who's on your team?**

Name of Team Member	Type of Help They Can Best Provide
1.	1.
2.	2.
3.	3.
4.	4.
5.	5.
6.	6.
7.	7.

Chapter 6

Engage in the 'reflect–digest–act–wait–decide' process

Overview

In this chapter, I discuss the importance of encouraging yourself to use the time after every self-help session to reflect on what you have learned from it, to digest this learning and, if relevant, to experiment with ways of implementing this learning in several different ways. After a reasonable amount of time, you can decide whether or not you need another self-help session. This is a feature of what has been called 'One-at-a-Time Therapy' (OAATT). In this way of working, the client is informed at the outset that the therapist will work hard with them to address the issue for which they have sought help and that they may have further sessions which they can only book one at a time, as made clear in the name given to this version of SST.

'Reflect–digest–act–wait–decide'

In 1990, BBC television launched a TV programme called *Masterchef* hosted by Lloyd Grossman where, in each programme, three contestants cooked for a panel of three judges, chaired by Grossman. Before announcing the winner, Grossman would say, 'We have deliberated, cogitated and digested and have come to our conclusion', which became his catchphrase.[1] When it

---

1 www.youtube.com/watch?v=LLdaa1oloRw

becomes clear that you will need several self-help sessions, take a leaf out of Lloyd Grossman's book and engage in a process at the end of which you can say the following: 'I have reflected on the session that I have had with myself, digested what I learned from it, took action based on this digested learning, waited to see what happened and made a decision as to whether or not to have a further session with myself.'

Reflect and digest

In this complex, fast-paced world with easy access to mobile phones, you may have to encourage yourself to stop and reflect on your experiences before making informed decisions. This principle particularly applies to self-help therapy. Once you have brought a self-help session to a close, reflect on and digest what you learned from the session. This may be done privately or with trusted, supportive others (see Chapter 5). Reflection involves you finding a quiet place and thinking about what you learned and how you may use this learning to address your nominated problem more effectively. Digestion takes reflection a step further and involves seeing how your learning can be applied more widely in your life (e.g. how you can apply what you learned to other situations) or how it links with principles that you hold dear.

Take action

Once you have understood your problem and chosen a solution based on that understanding, you need to take action and implement this solution to your nominated problem and, if necessary, apply it to other problems. You can also experiment with other related solutions that you may have thought about while in the reflection and digestion stage.

Wait

At times in the self-help process, it is useful to let things settle down and let time pass to assess the impact of the work you have done in the previous session. At the end of the process, letting time pass is particularly useful to determine what you have achieved before resuming self-therapy if needed.

Make a decision

The value of OAATT lies in the fact that the client knows that they can come back for another session if they need to. Knowing this means that they may not take up this offer, particularly if they are doing well. If not, they can choose to come back at a time convenient to them. Applying this to self-help, once you have solved your problem and maintained your gains (see Chapter 14), you know that you can always resume self-therapy, but it might be useful to take a break from such work so that you don't get stale and can resume self-therapy, if necessary, with renewed vigour.

In the next chapter, I will discuss the importance of focusing on one problem at a time when you launch self-therapy. Again, doing so will help you get the most out of the process.

Chapter 7

Develop a problem focus

Overview

In this chapter, I will discuss the importance of focusing on your problems. After making a list of all your problems that you would like to help yourself with, I suggest that it is important to put them in the order that you would like to tackle them. Then you need to focus on your problems one at a time. I suggest that you call the problem that you have selected your 'nominated' problem. In this chapter, I distinguish between two types of problems: problems resulting from facing adversity and problems resulting from avoiding facing the adversity.

Select one problem to address

When you embark on the process of helping yourself with your problems, at the outset it is useful to make a list of the problems that you want to deal with. After you have done this, I suggest that you put them in the order in which you want to tackle them. This order may change over the course of self-help, but having an order suggests the problem with which you want to start. As I have already mentioned, I call this problem the 'nominated' problem. If you have several problems, your nominated problem might be the one that you are most concerned with currently, the one which might be easiest to tackle (if different), or the one which might give you the most sense of hope and encouragement if you are successful in dealing with it.

Keep your focus on your nominated problem

Unless there is a good reason to do otherwise, keep your focus on your nominated problem until you have solved it. Otherwise, you will end up juggling several problems at once with predictable consequences. It would be like beginning to paint your kitchen, then, before finishing, moving to paint your dining room and then on to painting your bedroom. You will have several partially painted rooms with none finished. Thus, moving from your nominated problem before you have solved it to focus on a second problem and then a third problem would have the same result – several partially addressed problems with none solved.

So, what would constitute good reasons to shift your focus from your nominated problem to another problem? There are two major reasons for doing so. First, in the course of working on your nominated problem, if another listed problem 'flares up' and pre-occupies you to the extent that you do not have sufficient mental space to devote to your nominated problem, then it is a good idea to switch focus to the second problem which then becomes your current nominated problem. Stay focused on the new nominated problem until you have solved it, as before. The second reason for switching focus is when you have made a reasonable attempt to solve your nominated problem, and it just has not worked. Then it makes sense to switch your focus to a second problem. Alternatively, failing to help yourself with your original nominated problem is a sign to seek help from a professional therapist or counsellor who may bring a fresh pair of eyes to the situation.

To reiterate, keep your focus on your nominated problem until you have solved it and then move to the next problem on your list.

Two categories of emotional problems

In my view, there are two categories of emotional problems that people have. The first category is when people encounter an adversity and respond with one or more troublesome emotions as a result of this encounter. I will discuss how to understand and formulate this problem category in Chapter 8. The second category occurs as a result of people's attempts to avoid the adversities and/or the troublesome emotions that they would experience if they faced the situations in which the adversity is deemed to exist. I will discuss how to understand and formulate this problem category in Chapter 9.

Understand and formulate emotional problems based on people's responses to adversity

Overview

In this chapter, I will focus on emotional problems that are based on people's responses to adversity. I call such problems category A problems to distinguish them from problems based on avoidance which I call category B problems. If your problem is a category A problem, I will help you to understand it and formulate it in this chapter.

Introduction

Before you can address your problem and develop potential solutions, in my view, you need to understand and formulate the problem. There are two ways of formulating your nominated problem, and although I will describe them separately in this chapter, they are linked. The first way is that which feels most natural to you as it is based on your own experience of the factors involved. The second way is based on professional ways of understanding emotional problems. Such frameworks bring together important factors which should include the factors that you experience, but also factors that you may not have thought about.

In single-session therapy (SST), a client is encouraged to state their understanding of their nominated problem and is asked if they would be interested in hearing their therapist's professional understanding of the same problem. In SST, the therapist and the client work together to come up with a shared understanding of the nominated problem before proceeding to address it. What I will do in this book is to share my professional understanding of common emotional problems for which people typically seek help from therapists or from themselves. You are free to take as much (or as little) from this understanding as makes sense to you in the course of your self-help sessions.

Understanding category A problems: emotional problems based on responses to adversity

Before I discuss this category of emotional problems, let me make it clear what I mean by the term 'adversity'.

What is an adversity?

For me, an adversity is something that you find unpleasant and a challenge. This is often subjective and involves you making an inference about the situation in which you find yourself.

Inferences

You will understand the subjective nature of inferences by considering the point that, in the same situation, different people find different aspects of the situation challenging. For example, imagine a situation where you are in a group of people discussing a particular topic, and the group leader has the habit of asking specific people for their views on the topic. Here is a range of adversity-related inferences experienced by different people in the group:

- The group leader will ask me for my opinion, and when I give it, people will think that what I have to say is stupid.
- The group leader will ask me for my opinion, and I will have to say that I don't have one. Others will be distinctly unimpressed.

- The group leader will ask me for my opinion, and I will blush.
- The group leader will not ask me for my opinion because he thinks that what I have to say is of no interest to the group.
- If I say something foolish in the group, people will ridicule me behind my back.

Please note the following about the above adversity-related inferences:

1. As I emphasised earlier, they occur in the same situation.
2. They each focus on a subjective aspect of the situation.
3. They are inferences in that they go beyond the data at hand. They may prove to be true or false, but they need to be examined against past and present evidence.

Assume temporarily that your inference is true. My view is that it is therapeutically important for you to assume temporarily that your inference is true and deal with that eventuality. Let me show you what I mean. Let's take the case of the person who predicts that they will blush if asked for their opinion by the group leader. If this happens (i.e. they do blush), it is clearly an adversity for the person. However, if the person is not asked for their opinion by the group leader, then although they will be relieved (they were not asked, and therefore they did not blush), the next time they are in a similar situation, they will probably make the same inference (I will be asked, and I will blush). Indeed, during the group event, they will be guided by their adversity-related inference and if dealing with this adversity is a problem for them (e.g. they will be anxious before the group convenes and while they are in the group), they need to help themself to deal with it because it could happen. As such, let me underscore the following advice:

> **Assume temporarily that the problem-related adversity is true. Then deal with it.**

Personal example. Let me give you a personal example to illustrate my point. During my childhood and teenage years, I used to have a very bad stammer and was anxious about speaking in front of a group in case I stammered. In the second year of grammar school, we had speech and elocution classes with the headmaster once a week, and at the end of the class he would call upon a pupil to stand in front of the class and read a paragraph of text three times. First, they were to read it using their own accent, then in a Welsh accent and finally in a Scottish accent. There were 35 boys in the class and thus this happened over 35 weeks. On each occasion, I experienced intense anxiety. My inference was: 'Today the headmaster will call on me, and I will stammer badly in front of my classmates.' As it happened, I was the only pupil not to be selected. My adversity did not come to pass, but this did not help me at all. Why? Because at the end of the year, I was still anxious about the prospect of stammering badly in front of a group. I guess the headmaster did not select me because he knew I would stammer badly in front of the group and he wanted to spare me this. If he had told me that at the outset, he would have spared me weeks of intense anxiety, but, and this is the important point, I would still have been anxious about the prospect of stammering badly in front of groups. What I needed was someone to help me assume temporarily that I would be selected and I would stammer badly in front of the class and then help me to deal with this adversity.

This is why my approach to dealing with an adversity is to help you to learn to face the adversity head-on and to learn to deal with it, rather to encourage you to think that it won't happen or it won't be as bad as you think it is. However, please bear in mind that this is my view. Only make use of it if you think that it will help you.

Common emotional problems in response to adversity

In my experience, there are eight major emotional problems for which people seek help. Table 8.1 lists the main broad adversity themes that feature in people's problems and the main troublesome disturbed emotional responses to these adversities.

Table 8.1 lists two terms that require explanation. The term 'personal domain' refers to anything or anyone that we hold dear

Table 8.1 **Common emotional problems and broad adversity themes**

Broad Adversity Theme in Relation to the Personal Domain	Emotional Problem
• Threat	• Anxiety
• Loss • Failure • Undeserved plight (to self or others)	• Depression
• Moral code violation • Failure to abide by moral code • Hurting others	• Guilt
• Falling very short of ideal • Others negatively evaluate self	• Shame
• Self more invested in relationship than is the other • Relationship rule violation (other treats self badly and undeservedly)	• Hurt
• Rule violation • Threat to self-esteem • Frustration	• Unhealthy anger
• Other poses threat to one's relationship • Uncertainty in relation to this threat	• Unhealthy jealousy
• Other has something that self prizes but does not have	• Unhealthy envy

to us. This might be a person, a physical object or an idea. The more central these are within our domain, the more likely we are to experience problems if these are threatened or we lose them, for example. The term 'broad adversity theme' refers to a very general category of adversity rather than a 'specific adversity theme' that is more relevant to a person's problem or specific adversities that appear in specific examples of this problem Thus, taking my personal example (see above), my specific adversity theme was 'stammering in front of a group', and the broad adversity theme is 'threat' to my personal domain.

Formulating your nominated category A problem

I mentioned earlier in this chapter that in SST the therapist and the client come to a joint formulation of the client's nominated problem. This involves them using both the client's understanding of the problem and the therapist's understanding. I suggest this as a way forward in self-help therapy informed by SST.

Formulating your nominated problem: use your own understanding

In this section, I will begin by focusing on your formulation of your nominated problem (see the first section of Table 8.2).

What you do here is write down in your own words your formulation of your problem as you currently see it. In the personal example that I discussed earlier, if I had been asked for my formulation, I would have said, 'I am anxious about stammering in public.' If you look at Table 8.2, you will see that it is divided into three sections. Your task at this point is to write your formulation of your nominated problem in Section 1. Do this before you read the following section of the chapter.

Formulating your nominated problem: the REBT problem formulation framework

In this section, I will help you to formulate your nominated problem using professional constructs. In this chapter I discuss how to formulate a category A problem where you experience a disturbed emotion in response to the presence of an adversity. Then, in the next chapter, I will discuss how to formulate a category B problem which, as I explained earlier, is based on your avoidance of the adversity. The professional constructs that I bring to this book are informed by an approach to therapy

Table 8.2 **Formulating your nominated problem informed by your own understanding and by professional constructs (in this case REBT)**

Section 1: Your Formulation of Your Nominated Problem Based on Your Own View

In the space below write down your own formulation of your nominated problem as you currently see it, using your own words.

| |
| |

Section 2: Formulating Your Nominated Problem Informed by Professional Constructs (in this case REBT)

Situations in which you experience your problem	
Your main troublesome emotion experienced in the above type of situations	
How you act or tend to act when you experience the troublesome emotion listed above	
How you think when you experience the troublesome emotion listed above	
The main adversity in your problem	

Section 3: Taking the Best from the Above Sections, State Your Formulation of Your Problem That You Will Work with Going Forward

| |
| |

known as Rational Emotive Behaviour Therapy (REBT), a form of Cognitive Behaviour Therapy (CBT).

Formulating a category A problem

As I pointed out above, a category A problem outlines a person's problematic emotional response to an adversity that the person actually encounters or thinks that they have encountered. Thus, if you have an emotional problem about being criticised, you will experience this problem when you actually have been criticised, when you think that you have been criticised and when you predict that you will be criticised. Remember the advice that I gave you earlier in this chapter: "Assume temporarily that your problem-related adversity is true." Doing this will help you to deal with the adversity.

Identify five major components when formulating a category A problem

Formulating a category A problem is based on identifying the following five components:

1. the type of situations in which you experience your problem
2. your main troublesome emotion experienced in the above type of situations
3. how you act or tend to act when you experience the troublesome emotion listed above
4. how you think when you experience the troublesome emotion listed above
5. what you were most disturbed about in the above type of situations. This is known as the main adversity theme.

You can use the above five-component schema in the appropriate place in Table 8.2. When you have done so, I recommend that you put these five elements together in narrative form (see Table 8.3 for an example later in this chapter). Let me discuss these components one at a time.

Identify the type of situations in which you experience your problem. Here you need to make a list of all the situations in which you experience your nominated problem. Here are some questions that you might find helpful:

- In which physical situations does the problem occur?
- What people tend to be present when you experience your problem?

Identify your main troublesome emotional response to the above adversity theme. When you come to identify the main troublesome emotion featured in your nominated problem, you may find this easy, or you may struggle with it. You also may do several problematic things when attempting to identify your main troublesome emotion.

- First, you may list several emotions rather than just your one main troublesome emotion. You may indeed experience several troublesome emotions in the situations you find problematic, but each of these emotions is likely to be about a different adversity, and you may end up confused. When you focus on your one main troublesome emotion, you increase your chances of identifying your main adversity theme, which is what you need to do.
- You may identify your most troublesome emotion but do so in very vague terms. Thus, you may say that you feel 'bad', 'upset' or 'out of sorts'. It is not clear to which specific emotions these emotions may refer and thus they should be avoided. The precise identification of your main troublesome emotion will help you identify other components of your nominated problem and thus if you need help in doing so, you may find consulting Table 8.1 presented earlier in this chapter useful. This table lists the main eight troublesome emotions for which people seek help either from themselves or from helping professionals. So, if you listed 'feeling bad' as your most troublesome emotion, then ask yourself which of the eight emotions listed in the table best describes what you

mean by 'feeling bad'. Table 8.1 also lists the broad adversity theme, which may help you to identify the main adversity theme involved with your nominated problem.

- You may think that you have identified your main troublesome emotion, but you may list an inference or an attitude towards yourself instead.

Examples of emotions that are inferences are as follows: 'I felt criticised', 'I felt rejected' and 'I felt blindsided'. Thus, when you say, 'I felt criticised', you are referring to an inference that you have made about the behaviour of another person who you think rightly or wrongly has criticised you and are saying that this inference is an emotion when it clearly isn't. If criticism is the main adversity theme of your nominated problem, then you need to ask yourself which one of the eight troublesome emotions listed in Table 8.1 describes your feelings about being criticised.

An example of a suggested emotion that is an attitude towards yourself is as follows: 'I felt like a bad person.' As you can see, this statement does not put forward one of the eight troublesome emotions outlined in Table 8.1. Rather it demonstrates an attitude towards yourself (i.e. you think that you are a bad person). You can then use this attitude to identify your main troublesome emotion as follows: 'When I think that I am a bad person for being criticised (for example), my main troublesome emotion is......' Then select one of the emotions in Table 8.1 that best approximates to your emotion.

Identify how you act or tend to act when you experience the troublesome emotion listed above. There are two important points to bear in mind here. The first point is that we are talking about behaviour that accompanies your main troublesome emotion. The second point refers to the difference between an overt action and an action tendency. When you experience an urge to act, you have a choice. First, you can either act on that urge, in which case you have transformed your action tendency into overt action. Second, you can decide not to act on the urge, in which case you are left with the action tendency. This distinction is important since change comes about from you recognising that you have an urge to act in a dysfunctional way but choosing not to act in that way, but rather to act in a functional way.

Behaviour that accompanies your main troublesome emotion tends to be dysfunctional or unconstructive in a number of ways. Thus, it tends to:

* interfere with your constructive goals and purposes
* be largely detrimental to your relationships
* yield short-term and long-term harmful results for you and
* help maintain rather than resolve your problem.

Identify how you think when you experience the troublesome emotion listed above. There are also two points to bear in mind here. First, such thinking tends to be quite distorted and skewed to the negative. Thus, when you are anxious, you tend to think in ways that magnify the nature of the threat you are facing and reduce your sense that you can deal with the threat. You may think that such thoughts are realistic, but they are not. They are coloured by your main troublesome emotion. Second, if you try to stop yourself from thinking such thoughts, they will tend to proliferate. So, as we will see, accepting such thoughts is a prelude to constructive change.

Identify your main adversity theme. This is what you are most disturbed about in the type of situations listed above. As it occurs in several situations, this theme will be general in nature. You may find this adversity theme easy to identify, but if not I suggest the following:

* Take the main troublesome emotion listed above (e.g. anxiety) and use it in a question such as 'What do I find most "anxiety-provoking" about these situations?'
* Take your main troublesome emotion listed above (e.g. anxiety) and then refer to Table 8.1, which lists the broad adversity theme that is associated with this emotion. Then, take the

broad adversity theme and ask yourself a question such as 'What do I find most threatening about these situations?'[1]

• Focus on the situations in which you experience your problem and ask yourself a question such as 'What one ingredient would I need for me not to experience my troublesome emotion in the situations outlined?' The opposite of this ingredient will often be the main adversity theme. Let me illustrate this by taking the example of Naomi to be discussed below. She is depressed in situations in which she submits work to her boss, and he says anything negative about her work. When she asked herself the question, 'What ingredient would I need not to be depressed in these situations?', Naomi responded, 'Knowing that I am doing as good a job as I can do.' The opposite of this is: 'I am not doing as good a job as I could do', which is her main adversity theme.

An example: the case of Naomi

Let me provide an example of how to formulate a category A problem by using the example of Naomi, who I briefly introduced at the end of Chapter 2. If you recall, Naomi's nominated problem was her difficulty in dealing with criticism. Using the above schema, which is informed by the professional constructs of Rational Emotive Behaviour Therapy (REBT), Naomi formulated her problem, which is outlined in Table 8.3.

Arriving at a workable formulation of the nominated problem based on both formulations previously made

Once you have formulated your category A problem from your own perspective and from a professional perspective, you should arrive at a final formulation based on both of these formulations. You may decide to go with your own formulation, or you may decide to go with the professional formulation. However, you may

---

1 This question of course applies when the main troublesome emotion is anxiety.

Table 8.3 Naomi's formulation of her nominated problem informed by her own understanding and by professional constructs

Section 1: Your Formulation of Your Nominated Problem Based on Your Own View
In the space below write down your own understanding of your nominated problem as you currently see it, using your own words.

> *I have problems dealing with my boss's feedback about my submitted work.*

Section 2: Formulating Your Nominated Problem Informed by Professional Constructs

Situations in which you experience your problem	*When I submit my work to my boss for evaluation and he says anything negative about it*
Your main troublesome emotion experienced in the above type of situations	*I feel depressed*
How you act or tend to act when you experience the troublesome emotion listed above	*Initially I feel like giving in my notice, but later I resolve to devote all my spare time to doing the next piece of work perfectly*
How you think when you experience the troublesome emotion listed above	*I'll never do as well as I can do*
The main adversity theme in your problem	*I am not doing as good a job as I could do*

Putting the above formulation in narrative form: *Whenever I submit my work to my boss and he says anything negative about it, I think that I am not doing as good a job as I could do. When this happens, I feel depressed and think that I will never do as well as I can do and feel like giving in my notice. Later, I resolve to spend all my spare time making sure that I do the next piece of work perfectly.*

Section 3: Taking the Best from the Above Sections State Your Formulation of Your Problem That You Will Work with Going Forward

> *I get depressed whenever I don't live up to my own potential. I get reminded of this whenever my boss points out that I have done something wrong or could do better, and I spend all my time trying to prevent this from happening.*

decide to develop a final formulation using both formulations. Do this in whatever way that makes sense to you. Whatever you decide to do, your final formulation should be the one you use in self-help going forward.

In the next chapter, I will concentrate on helping you to understand and formulate problems that are based on avoidance.

Chapter 9

Understand and formulate problems based on avoidance

Overview

In this chapter, I will focus on problems that are based on people's avoidance of adversity and the troublesome emotions that they would experience if they did face the adversity. I call such problems category B problems to distinguish them from problems based on people's responses to adversity which, as I discussed in the previous chapter, I call category A problems. If your problem is a category B problem, I will help you to understand it and formulate it.

Understanding category B problems: problems based on avoidance of adversity and/or of troublesome emotional responses to this adversity

Perhaps the most common way in which we deal with adversity is to avoid it. The reason we do this is to spare us the emotional pain of the moment. This is fine if we take the time to reflect on how to deal with the adversity constructively. However, it becomes a problem if avoidance becomes the typical way we deal with problems.

It is important to remember that avoidance does not help us to deal with adversity. It is the main reason why we unwittingly maintain our problems. Let me reiterate that the best way of addressing our problem is to prepare to face the adversity, to face it and learn to deal constructively with it, and this book is based on this principle.

Table 9.1 lists common signs that a person's emotional problem is based on avoidance of the adversity. As Table 9.1 shows, different avoidance strategies are employed depending on the adversity to be avoided.

Table 9.1 **Signs that a person's emotional problems are based on avoidance**

Adversity Theme in Relation to the Personal Domain	Signs of Avoidance
• Threat	• Avoiding threat • Not taking sensible risks • Feeling stuck in a rut
• Loss	• Staying away from things or people that are wanted in case of subsequent loss
• Failure	• Only doing things where success is guaranteed • Having a sense that one is not fulfilling one's potential
• Undeserved plight (to self or others)	• Avoiding bad news
• Moral code violation	• Checking constantly that one has not done the wrong thing • Seeking reassurance from others that one has done the right thing
• Hurting others	• Checking constantly that others are OK • Seeking reassurance from others that one has not hurt their feelings • Not asserting self • Putting others first • Not doing what one wants in case others don't approve

Table 9.1 **Cont.**

• Falling very short of ideal	• Not taking sensible risks • Only doing things where success is guaranteed
• Others negatively evaluate self	• Staying away from others • Only showing a positive public face • Denying or covering up weaknesses
• Self more invested in relationship than is the other	• Keeping relationships superficial • Not taking risks where one can have one's feelings hurt • Cutting oneself off from others
• Relationship rule violation (other treats self badly and undeservedly)	• Not asserting self
• Rule violation	• Trying to persuade self that the violation does not matter when it does
• Threat to self-esteem	• Avoiding threat
• Frustration	• Trying to ensure that one is never frustrated
• Other poses threat to one's relationship	• Avoiding threat and encouraging partner to avoid threat
• Uncertainty in relation to this threat	• Seeking reassurance from the other • Checking constantly for the presence or absence of threat to one's relationship
• Other has something that self prizes but does not have	• Trying to equalise things so that one has what the other has or spoiling things for the other • Putting down those who one envies or criticising them

General signs of emotional problems based on avoidance

There are several general signs that a person's problems are based on avoidance. These signs are present no matter what the adversity is. I will discuss two here: procrastination and substance misuse.

Procrastination

We all procrastinate at times. When procrastination is problematic, the person routinely avoids dealing with something that it is in their interests to do at a time when it is important to them to do it. Procrastination is a sign that you are avoiding an adversity in your life. You may know what this adversity is, but if your procrastination is chronic, you have trained yourself to avoid something, and you may no longer know what it is. When you routinely procrastinate, you may then condemn yourself for doing so, and, if so, you now have three problems: i) the original adversity that you would have an emotional problem about were you to face it (i.e. a category A problem), ii) your routine avoidance of the adversity in your category A problem (i.e. a category B problem), and iii) your self-condemnation about your avoidance.

Substance misuse

People often use substances to deal with adversities. Common substances that people use are alcohol, drugs and food. Substance misuse occurs when people make routine use of their substance or substances of choice. In my view, substance misuse is a form of avoidance since the person is avoiding dealing with the adversity without the tranquillising effects of the substance.

It is important to distinguish between 'intent' and 'consequence' when discussing such use. When a person uses a substance to deal with an adversity, they intend to deal with it without emotional pain. A typical example is someone who drinks alcohol to calm their nerves before giving a talk.

The consequence of such use may be that the person does deal with their adversity without experiencing emotional pain, but there are other consequences. First, the person, as we have discussed, may become dependent on the substance to deal with the adversity. Second, the use of the substance may affect their behaviour in unintended ways. Thus, the person may become intoxicated and display this while giving their talk. Third, the person may use the substance to deal with other adversities. Fourth, the person may experience a variety of negative health-related consequences as a result of their substance misuse. Finally, the person may become generally 'addicted' to the use of their substance of choice, and this 'addiction' may have highly negative consequences on their work and on their relationships.

Well-meaning helpers try to persuade people to address their substance misuse because of the consequences of such misuse as outlined above. However, the person's behaviour may be guided by their intentions rather than by their consequences, and it is these that need to be addressed, as I will presently discuss.

Before leaving this topic, it is important to recognise that people who develop substance misuse issues tend to deny to others that they misuse their substance of choice. They may also engage in self-deception to prevent themselves from taking ownership of their problem. Given that I pointed out in Chapter 2 that this book is only for people who recognise that they have a problem that they wish to address, it is unlikely that you will use this book if this applies to you. Why? Because not only do you think that you do not have a substance misuse problem, but your use (or misuse) of the substance will also lead you to think that you don't even have a category A problem. Thus, if you use alcohol to calm your nerves while giving a talk, it may work in the short term. If it didn't, you would not use the substance.

In short, only use this book if i) you recognise that you have a category B problem and ii) this is covering up a category A problem that you wish to address and you are willing to do so without using your substance of choice. A tall order, maybe, but one that you can implement.

Formulating a category B problem

To recap, by a category B problem I mean a problem you have that is largely characterised by avoidance of situations in which, if you faced them, you would encounter a main adversity theme and would experience a main troublesome emotion about this adversity (i.e. a category A problem). You may wish to avoid the adversity, the troublesome emotion or both. I mentioned two major examples of such avoidance when it becomes chronic. These were procrastination and substance misuse. However, avoidance can occur in a myriad different ways, and if you have concluded that you have a category B problem, then you need to identify your major form of avoidance.

Identify six major components when formulating a category B problem

Formulating a category B problem is based on identifying six components:

1. Identify your major forms of avoidance.
2. Ask yourself what you are avoiding.
3. Do a cost–benefit analysis of facing what you have been avoiding or continuing to avoid it.
4. Understand the factors that explain your avoidance.
5. Deal with the factors that explain your avoidance.
6. Your category B problem is now a category A problem. Refer to how to deal with a category A problem in Chapter 8.

Let me deal with these components one at a time. See Table 9.2 for a form that you can use when dealing with a category B problem.

Identify your major forms of avoidance

If you have decided that your nominated problem is characterised by avoidance, then be clear with yourself when you are in avoidant mode. In Table 9.2, list the ways in which you avoid encountering what would be a category A problem where you would face situations in which your main adversity theme featured and where you would experience a main troublesome emotion.

Ask yourself what you are avoiding

The next step is for you to ask yourself what you are avoiding and list this in Table 9.2. As I said earlier, this will be a situation-related

Table 9.2 **Dealing with a category B problem based on avoidance**

List your major forms of avoidance	
What are you avoiding?	
List the advantages of continuing to avoid what you have been avoiding	
List the disadvantages of continuing to avoid what you have been avoiding	
Understand the factors that explain your avoidance	
Deal with the factors that explain your avoidance	

Your category B problem is now a category A problem. Refer to how to deal with a category A problem in Chapter 8.

adversity, a troublesome emotion that you would experience if you faced the adversity or both. If you struggle with this task, here are some questions to help you:

- 'What would have to be taken away from the situations you are currently avoiding that would enable you to stop avoiding them?' Your response will be probably your main adversity theme.
- 'What troublesome emotion would you have to not experience in order for you to stop avoiding the situations you are currently avoiding?' Your response will probably be your main troublesome emotion.

Do a cost–benefit analysis of facing what you have been avoiding or continuing to avoid it

It is important that you commit yourself to dealing with your avoidance-based problem and this involves deciding to do so based on carrying out a cost–benefit analysis of two choices: facing what you have been avoiding or continuing to avoid it. I show you how to do this in Table 9.2. If you genuinely decide in favour of the latter, then your self-help stops at this point. However, if you decide to continue, then the next step is understanding the factors that underpin your avoidance.

Understand the factors that explain your avoidance

Unless you understand the factors that explain why you have routinely avoided situations that are important to face, then you will continue to avoid them even if you have previously decided to tackle your avoidance-based problem. You can promote such understanding in three ways:

- List the factors that *you* think explain your continuing avoidance.
- Consider what Rational Emotive Behavior Therapy (REBT) has to offer you on this point.
- Draw upon both.

How you explain your continuing avoidance. Based on the cost–benefit analysis you did above and your other reflections on the topic, which factors do you think explain your continuing avoidance? Write these factors down, ready to deal with them presently.

Contributions from REBT. On this point, REBT theory argues the following: i) It is not the presence of the situations or what you find aversive about these situations that explain your avoidance. Rather, your avoidance is explained by your attitude towards these situations and/or adversity. ii) It is not the experience of your troublesome emotion that explains your avoidance. Again, it is your attitude towards this emotion that explains it. Applying this point, you can ask yourself the following questions:

- 'What attitude do I have towards the situations and/or what I find aversive about them that explains my avoidance of them?'
- 'What attitude do I have towards the troublesome emotion that I would experience if I faced the adversity that explains why I avoid experiencing the emotion?'

In Table 9.3, I present four attitudes that underpin avoidance in these situations and I also present four attitudes that would help you to face rather than avoid. Take what you find valuable from REBT's contribution and ally it with what you have written in response to the questions above.

Draw upon both perspectives. As before, I suggest that you consider your views concerning why you avoid and REBT's perspective and then decide whether to go with one explanation or the other or to take what is best from both.

Deal with the factors that explain your avoidance

Once you have identified the factors that explain your avoidance, then you need to deal with them. Take these factors one at a time and ask yourself the following questions:

- What do I need to do or think that will help me to address this factor and overcome my avoidance?

Table 9.3 **Attitudes that lead to avoidance of situations, adversities and troublesome emotions and attitudes that promote facing them**

Attitudes that Lead to Avoidance of Situations, Adversities and Troublesome Emotions	Attitudes that Promote Facing Situations, Adversities and Troublesome Emotions
Rigid Attitude • 'I must not encounter the situation, adversity and/or troublesome emotion'	**Flexible Attitude** • 'I would prefer not to encounter the situation, adversity and/or troublesome emotion, but that does not mean that I must not do so. Indeed, facing them is the best way of addressing my emotional problem'
Awfulising Attitude • 'It would be terrible if I encountered the situation, adversity and/or troublesome emotion'	**Non-awfulising Attitude** • 'It would be bad if I encountered the situation, adversity and/or troublesome emotion, but it would not be terrible'
Discomfort Intolerance Attitude • 'I could not tolerate it if I encountered the situation, adversity and/or troublesome emotion'	**Discomfort Tolerance Attitude** • It would be hard for me to tolerate it if I encountered the situation, adversity and/or troublesome emotion, but I could tolerate it and I am going to do so if it is worth it to me'
Devaluation Attitude • 'It's bad if I encountered the situation, adversity and/or troublesome emotion and if I did I am bad/you are bad/life is bad'	**Unconditional Acceptance Attitude** • 'It's bad if I encountered the situation, adversity and/or troublesome emotion and if I did I am fallible/you are fallible /life is a complex mixture of good, bad and neutral'

• If I have proposed a thinking solution, how am I going to act on it?

Contributions from REBT. If you have decided to use one or more of the attitudes listed in Table 9.3 to help you face the situations, adversity and/or troublesome emotion you are avoiding, make a plan of what you are going to do to act on this healthy attitude. REBT also suggests that you use a principle that I have called 'challenging, but not overwhelming' here. This principle encourages you to face what you have been avoiding (using the factors that I have previously discussed) but to do so in a way that you currently find challenging. It urges you to refrain from taking action towards facing what you have been avoiding if doing so is currently overwhelming for you.

Draw upon your own views and REBT's contribution. Having identified your own views of how to deal with the factors that explain your avoidance and REBT's suggestions on this point, stand back and ask yourself: 'Am I going to proceed with my own views of how to deal with the factors that explain my avoidance or REBT's views or am I going to take what I consider the best of these views and integrate them?'

Your Category B Problem is Now a Category A Problem

If you follow the steps that I have outlined in this chapter and that you have listed in Table 9.2, then you should now be in a position to face your problem rather than avoid it. While this is a significant step and you should pat yourself on the back for making it, it is only half the story. For you now have to deal with the problem you have been avoiding for all this time, which is now an example of what I call a category A problem. That is, you will experience a troublesome emotion when you face the situations that you previously avoided because of the adversity that is either present in these situations or that you think is present in them.

What you do now is to treat the problem as a category A problem, which involves following the steps that I outlined for dealing with such problems in the previous chapter. After you have done that, you are ready to set goals which I will discuss in the following chapter.

Chapter 10

Set goals

Overview

Once you have understood and formulated your nominated emotional problem, you are now in a position to set goals concerning this problem. Thus, at this point, SST-influenced self-help becomes more future-oriented as you begin to think about what you would consider to be a good outcome from your self-help efforts. In this chapter, I will discuss two different types of goals: problem-related goals and session goals.

When focusing on problem-related goals – which can also be seen as outcome goals – I will discuss three varieties: i) self-set, ii) professionally informed and iii) goals where you bring together the best of the two previous varieties above into a reformulated goal. Setting session goals refers to the practice where every time you have a session with yourself you set a goal for that session. When focusing on session goals – which can also be seen as process goals – I will discuss the following issues: i) making your session goal meaningful; ii) making your session goals realistic, iii) basing your session goals on what you have already achieved in the self-help process, and iv) choosing an appropriate level of session goal specificity.

Setting problem-related goals

As the name suggests, a problem-related goal relates to a state where you no longer have the problem. This issue is more complicated than it seems, as we will presently see.

Self-set problem-related goals

A self-set problem-related goal is your view of what would have to exist for you to conclude that you no longer have the problem. It is couched in your own words and is free from the influence of professional constructs. The main advantage of a self-set goal is that you express it in your own words, and therefore they come from the heart. The more connected you are to a goal, the more likely you are to achieve it.

Express your goal as the presence of a positive state

The main disadvantage of a self-set goal occurs when it is expressed as the absence of something. You may recall that in Chapter 8 I discussed my anxiety about stammering in public. If asked at that time what my goal was concerning this problem, I would either have said, 'Not stammering in public', or 'Not feeling anxious about stammering in public'. You will see from both of these statements that they point to the absence of something ('*not stammering*' or '*not feeling anxious*'). This is problematic because good goals specify the presence of a healthy state rather than the absence of an unhealthy state.

In Chapter 8, I discussed the case of Naomi. In Table 8.3, Naomi formulated her problem in her own words: 'I have problems dealing with my boss's feedback about my submitted work.' Her self-set goal concerning this problem was: 'I want to respond to the boss's feedback about my submitted work in a constructive way.' As you can see, Naomi's goal does specify the presence of a healthy state (i.e. '*to respond constructively*').

Professionally informed problem-related goals

There are two ways in which your problem-related goal-setting can be informed by professional constructs. The first way, which comes from Cognitive Behaviour Therapy (CBT), involves using the acronym 'SMART' in your goal-setting. The second way involves you drawing upon your REBT-informed emotional problem formulation and using that to set a goal.

Be SMART in setting your problem-related goal

CBT encourages us to set goals that are: specific, meaningful, achievable, realistic and time-sensitive. Taking the first letter from each of these descriptors, we get the acronym SMART, which is easily remembered and can help you in your goal-setting. Use it if you think that it could enhance the chances that you will achieve your goal. I will now discuss each descriptor in turn.

Express your goal as specifically as possible. You will recall that Naomi set 'I want to respond to the boss's feedback about my submitted work in a constructive way' as a problem-related goal (see above). The difficulty with Naomi's goal is that it is vague. What precisely does 'respond in a constructive way' mean? Naomi probably has some idea what it is for her to respond constructively and therefore she should encourage herself to spell this out for herself. The importance of setting a specific goal resides in the fact that you are more likely to pursue a goal if it is specific than if it is vague.

Make your goal meaningful. The more meaningful what you want to achieve concerning your problem is to you, then the more likely you are to commit time and energy to work towards the goal and thus the more likely it is that you will achieve it. Examples of good questions you can ask yourself on this point are: 'How important is it to me to achieve this goal?' and 'Why is achieving the goal so important to me?' On this point, the more consistent your goal is with one of your core values, the more meaningful it is likely to be to you. So think of your core values when goal-setting.

Make your goal achievable. An achievable goal is one that is not only achievable in general, but one that you think you can achieve. This descriptor often has to be considered along with the time-sensitive descriptor (to be discussed later). If you set yourself a particular timeframe for achieving a goal, then you need to ask yourself whether you can achieve the goal within that timeframe.

Make your goal realistic. Sometimes a person sets a goal, and it is just not realistic. Using my personal example that I discussed in Chapter 8, where my problem was being anxious about stammering in front of others, if my goal were to be perfectly fluent in such circumstances, then that would not be realistic. More than fifty years on from that personal example, I am much more fluent in such settings but still stammer at times. Perfect fluency as a goal would have been unrealistic then, and it is unrealistic now.

Make your goal time-sensitive. This point reflects the timeframe in which you want to achieve your problem-related goal. Time is an important factor in both single-session therapy and self-help informed by SST. If you give yourself plenty of time to achieve your goal, then you will not use time effectively in pursuing the goal. However, if you give yourself insufficient time to achieve it, you are setting yourself up for failure, and you may become discouraged with self-help as a result. SST would argue that you give yourself sufficient time to pursue the goal in a committed way without putting too much pressure on yourself. Remember that the timeframe you choose may make an achievable goal unachievable.

Use the REBT problem-related goal-setting framework

Earlier in this book, I distinguished between a category A problem and a category B problem. I stated that a category A problem occurs in response to situations with which you struggle and to the adversities that are present, or you infer to be present, in these situations. By contrast, a category B problem occurs when you routinely avoid such adversity-related situations. I argued that dealing with a category B problem exposes you to the category A problem that you have been, in effect, avoiding and with which you still have to deal. In the final analysis, you will need to deal with your category A problem whether you have been routinely avoiding it or not.

In Chapter 8, I encouraged you to use the REBT problem formulation framework for category A problems. If you recall, this framework had five components:

• Identify the type of situations in which you experience your problem.
• Identify your main adversity theme.

- Identify your main troublesome emotional response to the above adversity theme.
- Identify how you act or tend to act when you experience the troublesome emotion listed above.
- Identify how you think when you experience the troublesome emotion listed above.

The REBT problem-related goal-setting framework is based on a very important idea and one that you need to consider seriously as you proceed with self-help. This idea states that as you have a problem dealing with adversity-based situations, you need to deal constructively with these situations and with the main adversity them if you are to solve your problem.

Consequently, you need to incorporate the first two components that appear in your problem formulation into your professionally informed, problem-related goal-setting framework.

Thus, the REBT problem-related goal-setting framework has the following five components:

- Identify the type of situations in which you experience your problem.
- Identify your main adversity theme.

  [Remember that you have already identified both the problem-related situations and the main adversity theme when using the REBT problem formulation framework. The following three components in the REBT problem-related goal-setting framework will be different from those identified in the REBT problem formulation framework.]
- Identify your main constructive emotional response to the above adversity theme.
- Identify how you will act or tend to act if you experience the constructive emotion listed above.
- Identify how you will think if you experience the constructive emotion listed above.

I suggest that you use Table 10.1 when setting goals, as it will make clear where your goal-setting focus needs to be.

Table 10.1 The REBT problem and problem-related goal-setting formulations

Identify the Situations in Which You Experience Your Problem:	
Identify the Main Adversity Theme:	
Troublesome Responses (PROBLEM)	**Constructive Responses (GOAL)**
Identify Your Main Troublesome Emotional Response to the Above Adversity Theme:	**Identify Your Main Constructive Emotional Response to the Above Adversity Theme:**
Identify How You Act or Tend to Act When You Experience the Troublesome Emotion Listed Above:	**Identify How You Will Act or Tend to Act If You Experience the Constructive Emotion Listed Above:**
Identify How You Think When You Experience the Troublesome Emotion Listed Above:	**Identify How You Will Think If You Experience the Constructive Emotion Listed Above:**

Let me discuss the final three components one at a time.

Identify your main constructive emotional response to the above adversity theme. What do I mean by a constructive emotional response to an adversity? First of all, let me reiterate that an adversity, by definition, is a negative event. As a result, you will have a negative emotional response to this negative event. REBT distinguishes between an unhealthy negative emotion (UNE) and a healthy negative emotion (HNE). A UNE is an emotion that is negative in feeling tone and unhealthy in effect. In this book, I refer to this as a troublesome emotion and it is the emotional component of your nominated emotional problem.

By contrast, an HNE is an emotion that again is negative in feeling tone, but this time it is healthy in effect. In this book, I refer to this as a constructive emotion and, from an REBT perspective, it is the emotional component of your problem-related goal. Table 10.2 lists both troublesome emotions and their constructive alternatives in response to broad adversity themes.

Using Table 10.1, having reiterated i) the situations in which you experience your problem, ii) the adversity theme that you find most troubling and iii) your main troublesome emotional response to that adversity, you should now write in your constructive emotional response to the same adversity. From an REBT perspective, this will serve as your emotional goal.

Identify how you will act or tend to act if you experience the constructive emotion listed above. Having set your emotional goal, you should now set your behavioural goal.

Again using Table 10.1, having reiterated how you act or tend to act when you experience your main troublesome emotions, you should now write in how you will act or tend to act if you experience the constructive emotional response to your adversity.

Behaviour that accompanies your main constructive emotion tends to be functional or constructive in several ways. Thus, it tends to:

- promote rather than interfere with your constructive goals and purposes
- be largely helpful rather than detrimental to your relationships

Table 10.2 **The REBT perspective on troublesome emotional responses to main adversities and alternative constructive emotional responses**

Broad Adversity Theme in Relation to the Personal Domain	Troublesome Emotion	Constructive Emotion
• Threat	• Anxiety	• Concern
• Loss • Failure • Undeserved plight (to self or others)	• Depression	• Sadness
• Moral code violation • Failure to abide by moral code • Hurting others	• Guilt	• Remorse
• Falling very short of ideal • Others negatively evaluate self	• Shame	• Disappointment
• Self more invested in relationship than is the other • Relationship rule violation (other treats self badly and undeservedly)	• Hurt	• Sorrow
• Rule violation • Threat to self-esteem • Frustration	• Unhealthy anger	• Healthy anger
• Other poses threat to one's relationship • Uncertainty in relation to this threat	• Unhealthy jealousy	• Healthy jealousy
• Other has something that self prizes but does not have	• Unhealthy envy	• Healthy envy

- yield constructive long-term results for you and
- help resolve rather than maintain your problem.

Identify how you will think if you experience the constructive emotion listed above. Such thinking tends to be realistic rather than distorted and skewed to the negative. Thus, when you are concerned rather than anxious, you tend to think in ways that realistically appraise both the nature of the threat you are facing and your perceived ability to deal with the threat.

An example: the case of Naomi

Let me provide an illustration of how to set a goal with respect to a category A problem by using the example of Naomi, who I briefly introduced at the end of Chapter 2 and discussed in Chapter 8. If you recall, Naomi's nominated problem was her difficulty in dealing with criticism. Using the above schema, which as I have said is informed by the professional constructs of Rational Emotive Behaviour Therapy (REBT), Naomi set her goals as outlined in Table 10.3. This form reminds you what your problem is as well.

Problem-related goals drawn from the best of the self-set goals and professionally informed goals

You have now set goals from your own perspective and used a therapeutic framework (in this case, REBT) to set professionally informed goals. Your final task with respect to setting problem-related goals is to take the best from both sets of goals and set a final goal which you will then work with going forward. Now, you don't have to do this. You can work with your own goal or work with the professionally informed goal. The choice is yours. The important thing is that you are committed to the goal and can refer to it easily.

Table 10.3 **The REBT problem and problem-related goal-setting formulations: the case of Naomi**

Identify the Situations in Which You Experience Your Problem:	
Being criticised by my boss	
Identify the Main Adversity Theme:	
Not doing as good a job as I can do	
Troublesome Responses (PROBLEM)	**Constructive Responses (GOAL)**
Identify Your Main Troublesome Emotional Response to the Above Adversity Theme:	Identify Your Main Constructive Emotional Response to the Above Adversity Theme:
Depression	**Sadness**
Identify How You Act or Tend to Act When You Experience the Troublesome Emotion Listed Above:	Identify How You Will Act or Tend to Act If You Experience the Constructive Emotion Listed Above:
Either giving up or devoting all my spare time to do things perfectly	**Sticking with things and making sure I spend my spare time on non-work activities**
Identify How You Think When You Experience the Troublesome Emotion Listed Above:	Identify How You Will Think If You Experience the Constructive Emotion Listed Above:
I'll never do as well as I can do	**Understanding that I can realise my potential but not perfectly so**

Setting session goals

Having dealt with setting problem-related goals, in this section I will turn my attention to session goals. One of the features of SST is that it tends to treat a therapy session as a discrete event. This is particularly the case when both therapist and client have contracted to meet just once. In such cases, when goal-setting is discussed it makes sense for the therapist to ask the client what they would like to achieve from this session. Asking for a session goal is thus very different from asking for an end of therapy goal (e.g. 'What would you like to achieve by the end of therapy?'). As you might expect, a problem-related goal is closer to an end of therapy goal than to an end of session goal. Given that you are likely to have more than one session of self-help, I still suggest that you set a goal for each session so that you can make most effective use of every session you decide to have with yourself. In addition, the achievement of session goals may be seen as stepping stones to the achievement of your problem-related goal. In this way, you will be able to see what progress you are making towards your problem-related goal with your self-help efforts.

Issues to consider when setting session goals

In the section above, when discussing setting problem-related goals, I outlined certain factors that you need to consider when setting these goals. These were all predicated on the idea that you would probably not achieve your problem-related goal at the end of your first, and only, session of self-help. Let me be clear again that this book concerns how to undertake self-help that is informed by single-session therapy. It is not a book on single-session therapy. So, what are the issues to consider when setting session goals?

Make your session goal meaningful

There are a number of questions or statements that you can use when setting a meaningful session goal. You may find it helpful to see some options and choose a question or statement that you find most meaningful. Alternatively, the questions that I present below may inspire you to find a more meaningful question of your own.

- What do I want to achieve by the end of the session?
- If at the end of the session I achieved.........(fill in the blank), it would encourage me to go forward.
- If at the end of the session I thought it was a worthwhile session, what would I have achieved?
- What would I have achieved at the end of the session for me to conclude that I have taken a significant step forward?

Make your session goals realistic

One of the points that can be taken from SST is that the client is more likely to take something meaningful from the single session if both the client and therapist share realistic expectations about what can be achieved from the session. Here, it is easier to understand what is meant by realistic if we first consider what is meant by unrealistic. In SST, unrealistic goals are either goals that specify fundamental change at the end of a session or ones that specify very minimal change. Thus, realistic goals operate in the middle ground between these extremes. They are ambitions and may stretch the person, but they are within the person's capability to achieve.

Base your session goals on what you have already achieved in the self-help process

While change can occur in a one-shot deal, normally it occurs over time and this is likely to be the case with self-help directed to achieving problem-related goals. As such, it is best if session goals can be linked together. Thus, a good session goal is related to how you have done with respect to your previous session goal. Given that change is not always linear, it is quite feasible for you to set a session goal that focuses on why you may not have progressed as much as you wanted since the previous session that you had with yourself.

Choose an appropriate level of session goal specificity

The level of specificity of your session goal has more flexibility than the level of specificity of a problem-related goal since it may refer to several different factors. Thus, a session goal can refer to such matters as

- identifying my strengths and resources that will help me in achieving my problem-related goal

- understanding my problem from a professional perspective[1]
- developing a list of possible solutions to my problem
- developing an action plan that will help me to implement my chosen solution
- identifying potential obstacles to implementing my action plan and proposing ways of dealing with such obstacles.

As you can see from the above list, session goals tend to be more general than problem-related goals.

In the next chapter, I will discuss how you can address your nominated problem based on your formulation of it. This involves you searching for solutions that could, if implemented, help you to achieve your problem-related goal. The main focus of the chapter will be on helping you to select a solution that you think you can best use to address your problem effectively. In doing so, you will be encouraged to use your inner strengths and available external resources.

---

1 In this book, I am suggesting that you draw upon the insights of Rational Emotive Behaviour Therapy and use whatever seems useful to you from this professional framework. There are, of course, other frameworks that you might find useful.

Chapter 11

Address your problem by searching for a solution

Overview

The heart of the self-help process is addressing your problem. In particular, this involves you considering several solutions and choosing one which you can implement and which will help you to achieve your problem-related goal. In this chapter, I will first help you to list several such possible solutions from your own perspective and to choose the one that seems most likely to address your problem. Then, I will put forward REBT's view of what might constitute effective solutions to your problem. I then encourage you to select a solution to implement going forward. This might be your personal solution, the one suggested by REBT or an integrated solution based on what you judge to be the best of both of these perspectives. Whichever solution you select, it is important that you rehearse it to see if you can see yourself implementing it, making any suitable modifications to the chosen solution as a result of such rehearsal.

Focusing on solutions

There are two ways therapists approach single-session therapy (SST). The first involves the therapist and client working towards a shared formulation of the client's nominated problem and then selecting together the best possible solution to this problem.

I refer to this approach as the 'problem-based, solution-focused approach'.[1] The second approach involves the therapist and client bypassing problems instead of focusing on solutions to the problem. This is known as the 'solution-focused approach'.

What is a solution?

You will note that the 'problem-based, solution-focused approach' and the 'solution-focused approach' have one thing in common. They are both solution-focused. But what is meant by the term 'solution'? In my view, a solution is a means by which you render your problem a non-problem and/or deal effectively with your adversity theme. It also helps you to achieve your problem-related goal or take a significant step towards achieving it. Put graphically, we have:

Identifying and evaluating previous problem-solving attempts

It is very likely that you have tried to help yourself with your nominated problem before. Given this, it is important that you identify what you have already tried. This involves you listing your previous problem-solving attempts and evaluating their effects. This strategy comes from SST, which encourages clients and therapists to build upon what the client has done before rather than starting therapy with a blank slate.

In self-help informed by SST, the purpose of identifying and evaluating previous problem-solving attempts is twofold. First, it enables you to identify anything that has been helpful to you from these attempts and to use this in developing a solution. Second, it enables you to identify unhelpful problem-solving attempts and to refrain from using these going forward. You might find it helpful to use Table 11.1 to do this.

---

1 This book is an example of the 'problem-based, solution-focused approach'.

Table 11.1 List your previous attempts to deal with your problem and their outcome

List Your Problem	List All You Have Done in the Past to Deal with the Problem	Outcome

Throughout this book, I have suggested that you consider your own perspective on an issue before considering what a professional framework like Rational Emotive Behaviour Therapy (REBT) has to say on the subject. Having done this, you can then stand back and take and apply the best of both perspectives or remain either with your perspective or that suggested by the professional framework. I recommend that you proceed using the following order: i) focus on your perspective, ii) focus on the professional perspective and iii) take the best from both frameworks or choose to go with one framework or the other. My view is that this order is important because it enables you to focus on your views without these being unduly influenced by the professional perspective. This is particularly the case when developing potential solutions to your nominated problem.[2]

From problem to goal: using your own perspective to develop and evaluate solutions

As suggested above, I will begin by helping you to develop and evaluate potential solutions from your own perspective.

Listing potential solutions

To help you develop a list of possible solutions from your own perspective, I suggest that you use the professional problem and goal framework offered by REBT (see Table 11.2). This table replicates Table 10.1 but adds an important column in which you list the potential solutions to your problem. Let me take you through what you need to do in Table 11.2.

- First, again list the situations in which you experience the problem.
- Second, again list the main adversity theme which explains why these situations are problematic for you.

2 However, as mentioned before, feel free to approach this task in whatever order makes sense to you.

Table 11.2 Listing potential solutions based on prior problem-related and goal-setting formulations

Situations in Which the Problem Occurs					
	Main Adversity Theme				
		Problem	Potential Solutions (Possible Ways of Dealing with My Problem and Achieving My Problem-Related Goal)	Goal	
		Main Troublesome Emotion:		Constructive Emotion:	
		Behaviour (or Action Tendency) that Accompanies the Main Troublesome Emotion:		Behaviour (or Action Tendency) that Accompanies the Constructive Emotion:	
		Thinking that Accompanies the Main Troublesome Emotion		Thinking that Accompanies the Constructive Emotion	

- Third, in the left-hand column marked 'Problem' list the main troublesome emotion you experience and the behaviour (or action tendency) and thinking that accompany this main troublesome emotion.
- Fourth, in the right-hand column marked 'Goal' list the main constructive emotion you would experience in the adversity-related situations if you were to achieve your goal and how you would act and think when feeling that emotion. Here, it is important to keep to the front of your mind that your goal should ideally be how you would respond constructively in the situations where the adversity is present or is assumed by you to be present.

    So far, as noted above, the responses in Table 11.2 are the same as you listed in Table 10.1. The next step is new and important.
- In the middle column marked 'Solutions', you write down potential solutions. These are things that are within your control that will help you to deal with the adversity-related situation you have found problematic and to render this problem a non-problem. Alternatively, potential solutions enable you, in principle, to achieve your problem-related goal.

In doing this, you might like to consider drawing upon the following: i) the helpful components of previous problem-solving attempts, ii) the internal strengths that you listed earlier – reviewing these may suggest to you ways of addressing the problem that may solve it – and iii) the external resources that you identified earlier, particularly people who may help and/or support you in your problem-solving attempts. Also, you might like to consider the unhelpful components of previous problem-solving attempts and to ensure that these are not part of any of the potential solutions you have put in the 'Solutions' column in Table 11.2.

Evaluating each potential solution

Once you have listed all the solutions that you can think of, it is important that you evaluate each one. What you are looking for is a solution that you can implement that gives you the best chance of achieving your problem-related goal. You might find it helpful to use Table 11.3 in undertaking this task.

You will, of course, have your own criteria in mind when you evaluate each potential solution. However, you might find the following criteria helpful to you:

Effectiveness. The very definition of a solution is that it works. So when you consider your list of potential solutions, keep to the forefront of your mind the question: 'Which of my list of potential solutions is most likely to work in helping me to achieve my goal?'

Feasibility. However, just because a potential solution is likely to be the most effective, it does not follow that it will be the one you will select as there are other considerations to bear in mind. My mentor, Dr Albert Ellis, the creator of Rational Emotive Behaviour Therapy, used to quip that he had invented the most effective solution to help people give up smoking, but that nobody would ever use it. What a person should do to give up smoking is that every time they lit a cigarette, they should put the lit end into their mouth! Thus, for you to choose a solution, it needs to be feasible. This essentially means that you are prepared to use it.

An important aspect of the feasibility of a solution concerns the question: 'Can I integrate this solution into my life?' For example, if you decide to attend a gym five days a week to improve your physical fitness, you are more likely to use this solution if you live close to the gym than if you live far away from it. Unless you can integrate the solution into your life, my recommendation is not to select it.

Relationship to strengths. When evaluating a potential solution, it may be helpful if you think about whether or not the solution can be underpinned by one or more of the strengths that you previously identified. In my view, you are more likely to implement a solution and maintain its use if you can bring one or more of your key strengths to the situation.

Likely support from others. If you value the support of others in implementing your selected solution, then you may like to think about which of your listed solutions is likely to be supported by these others.

Table 11.3 Evaluating potential solutions to your nominated problem

	Potential Solution	Evaluation
1.		
2.		
3.		
4.		
5.		

Based on the above evaluation I have selected the following as my chosen solution:

Rehearse the solution and then if necessary make any changes to your chosen solution based on that rehearsal. Write the amended solution here:

Potential obstacles. In evaluating a possible solution, you might find it helpful to think about potential obstacles to you implementing it. If you cannot think of ways of dealing with an obstacle, you may wish to think twice about selecting that solution.

Selecting a solution

Having listed and evaluated your potential solutions, you should now be in a position to select the one that you think is the best based on your personal view, perhaps informed by the criteria that I have presented and discussed above. You will see that there is a space at the bottom of Table 11.3 to enter your chosen solution.

Therapists who work in SST encourage their clients to rehearse their chosen solution to see if there is a good experiential fit between the solution and how it feels to carry it out. One of the ways that you can do this is to try your chosen solution out in real life but in relatively unchallenging circumstances. The main reason for doing this is for you to see how you 'feel' enacting the solution. At this point, it is not to solve the problem. Please bear in mind one important point here. You will probably feel uncomfortable implementing the solution. Why? Because you are not used to doing it. It goes against the grain, and anything that goes against the grain will feel uncomfortable to do. So, while accepting that any new solution you try will feel uncomfortable, your goal is to judge whether or not you can see yourself carrying out the solution based on an action plan which I will discuss in the next chapter. If so, you may still want to 'tweak' the solution in some way. There is a space in Table 11.3 for you to enter your 'tweaked' solution.

Another way of judging the experiential fit of your chosen solution is to rehearse it in imagery. In doing so, you will feel less discomfort – as behavioural rehearsal of a new solution tends to yield more discomfort than imagery rehearsal – but it will enable you to judge whether you can see yourself putting the solution into practice. If your rehearsal of the solution leads you to dismiss the solution, then you will need to return to your solution list and select the next most feasible and effective solution and rehearse it as described above. However, if you can imagine yourself carrying out the solution (original or 'tweaked'), then you are ready to consider what REBT has to contribute to the search for a good solution to your problem.

From problem to goal: possible solutions from a professional perspective

Once you have selected a solution from your own perspective, you may wish to consider what solutions are available to you from a professional perspective – in this case, Rational Emotive Behaviour Therapy (REBT). In this section, I will outline REBT's position on what constitutes a problem and what would constitute a solution to this problem. This position is summarised in Table 11.4.

You will see from Table 11.4 that I have included material introduced in Chapter 10. This covers both the problem and the problem-related goal.

Viewing the problem from an REBT perspective, you experience your nominated problem in situations where your main adversity theme is present or deemed to be present. Your problem is characterised by a main troublesome emotion and when you experience this emotion, you will think in highly distorted ways and act (or tend to act) in dysfunctional ways. Concerning the problem-related goal, REBT argues that you develop a set of constructive emotional, behavioural and thinking responses to the adversity-based situations that you find problematic.

Table 11.4 also contains important information that specifies REBT's view concerning the role that attitudes play in determining both your problem and your problem-related goal. Concerning the latter point and highly relevant to the current focus on solutions, Table 11.4 shows the attitudes you need to develop towards your main adversity theme that will allow you to solve your problem, particularly if you act and think in ways that are consistent with such attitudes. What follows is a detailed delineation of these points.

Table 11.4 The REBT problem and problem-related goal-setting formulations with underlying attitudes

The Situations in Which You Experience Your Problem:	
The Main Adversity Theme:	
Rigid and Extreme Attitudes	**Flexible and Non-extreme Attitudes**
• Rigid Attitude (Preference plus Must)	• Flexible Attitude (Preference without Must)
• Awfulising Attitude (Bad plus Awful)	• Non-awfulising Attitude (Bad without Awful)
• Discomfort Intolerance Attitude (Struggle plus Intolerance)	• Discomfort Tolerance Attitude (Struggle plus Tolerance)
• Devaluation Attitude (It's Bad plus I Am/You Are/Life Is Bad)	• Unconditional Acceptance Attitude (It's Bad plus I am/You Are/Life Is Fallible/Complex)
Troublesome Responses (PROBLEM)	**Constructive Responses (GOAL)**
• Emotional	• Emotional
• Behavioural	• Behavioural
• Thinking	• Thinking

The role of attitudes in your problem and problem-related goal

As I have already mentioned, REBT is an approach within the cognitive-behavioural tradition of counselling and psychotherapy. This means that it focuses on thinking (cognition) and behaviour when considering both a person's problematic responses to adversity and what they need to change in their thinking and behaviour to respond constructively to the same adversity. REBT's distinctive contribution to CBT on this point states that our responses (emotive, behavioural and cognitive) to adversity depend on the attitudes that we hold towards this adversity. I have outlined these in Table 11.4 but will discuss them now.

The role of attitudes in your problem. REBT holds that when you respond problematically to adversity, you hold a rigid attitude and one or more extreme attitudes towards this adversity. Let me outline each of these attitudes in turn.

Rigid attitude. A rigid attitude has two components: i) *a preference component* whereby you prefer that the adversity not exist and ii) *a demand component* whereby you demand that it must not do so.

Awfulising attitude. An awfulising attitude has two components: i) *a badness component* whereby you evaluate the existence of the adversity as bad and ii) *an awfulising component* whereby you further evaluate its existence as awful.

Discomfort intolerance attitude. A discomfort intolerance attitude has two components: i) *a struggle component* whereby you note that it is difficult for you tolerate the discomfort that you are experiencing and ii) *an intolerance attitude* whereby you note that such discomfort is intolerable.

Devaluation attitude. A devaluation attitude can refer to self, other(s) or life. It has two components: i) *a negative evaluation of a part (of self, other(s), or life) component* and ii) *a devaluation of self, other(s) or life component* whereby you assign a global, negative devaluation of self, other(s) or life.

The role of attitudes in your problem-related goal. REBT holds that when you respond healthily to adversity, you hold a flexible attitude and one or more non-extreme attitudes towards this adversity. Let me again outline each of these attitudes in turn.

Flexible attitude. A flexible attitude has two components: i) *a preference component* whereby again you prefer that the adversity not exist and ii) *a non-demand component* whereby you recognise that it does not have to be so.

Non-awfulising attitude. A non-awfulising attitude has two components: i) *a badness component* whereby you evaluate the existence of the adversity as bad and ii) *an anti-awfulising component* whereby you recognise that its existence is not awful.

Discomfort tolerance attitude. A discomfort tolerance attitude has five components: i) *a struggle component* whereby you note that it is difficult for you tolerate the discomfort that you are experiencing; ii) *a tolerance attitude* whereby you note that such discomfort is tolerable; iii) *a worth it component* whereby you judge that the discomfort is worth bearing (if it is); iv) *a willingness component* whereby you assert that you are willing to commit to tolerating the discomfort; v) *a commitment component* whereby you commit yourself to doing so.

Unconditional acceptance attitude. An unconditional acceptance attitude can again refer to self, other(s) or life. It has two components: i) *a negative evaluation of a part (of self, other(s) or life) component* and ii) *an unconditional acceptance of self, other(s) or life component* whereby you accept self, other(s) or life as too complex to merit a global evaluation and composed of numerous positive and negative features.

While the holding of these flexible and non-extreme attitudes towards adversity characterise healthy ways of responding to the adversity, the development of these attitudes and the behaviours and thinking that accompany them are seen as solutions to the problem that enable you to achieve your problem-related goal.

From problem to goal: going forward with personal and professional solutions

Having formulated a solution from your own perspective and from a professional perspective, you are ready to do one of the following (see Table 11.5).

Table 11.5 **From problem to goal: going forward with personal and professional solutions**

Solution	
Personal	
Professional	
Integrated	

- Go forward based on the solution you formulated from your own perspective.
- Go forward based on the solution you formulated from the professional perspective you decided to use (in this case, REBT).
- Go forward based on integrating the personal and professional solutions.

Integrating personal and professional solutions

In this closing section of the chapter, I will focus on integrating personal and professional solutions. Here, your task is to consider both solutions, take what you consider is the best from each solution and put them together or integrate them. You may need to tweak elements to ensure that the different solutions fit well together. Then you can write down your integrated solution in the space for that purpose in Table 11.5.

Once you have chosen the solution which you want to take forward, and if you have not already done so, I suggest that you rehearse your chosen solution to see if there is a good experiential fit between the solution and how it feels to carry it out. I described how you can do this earlier in the chapter.

In the following chapter, I will discuss how you can develop an action plan to implement your chosen solution.

Chapter 12

Develop and implement an action plan related to your chosen solution

Overview

In this chapter, I will discuss what steps you need to consider when developing an action plan to implement your chosen solution concerning your nominated problem.

Then I will discuss matters to do with the implementation itself. As I have pointed out before, my view is that, for you to help yourself effectively, you need to face the main adversity theme which explains why you find various situations problematic and implement your chosen self-help as you do so. You need to be sensible as you implement your chosen solution, and I will discuss the 'challenging, but not overwhelming' concept in this context.

Design your action plan

An action plan is a broad plan which outlines what action you are going to take the objective of which is the achievement of your problem-related goal. This involves you facing situations where you think your main adversity theme will be present while experiencing a constructive emotion and acting and thinking in ways that are consistent with this emotion.

Components of an action plan

An action plan comprises several components:

- the *situations* that you find problematic and that you wish to face
- the *order* in which you plan to face each situation
- a *timetable* where you specify when you are going to face each situation
- the *solution*, duly modified to reflect the situation in which you are going to implement it
- a *feedback* session where you are going to evaluate your experience in implementing the solution and make any changes based on your experience
- clear *signposts* that tell you that you are on the way to achieving your problem-related goal
- a list of your *strengths and other helping resources* that you can make use of when striving to reach your signpost and later your problem-related goal
- a list of *possible obstacles* that you may encounter during the process of working towards the signpost and problem-related goal and a way of addressing them.

The importance of integrating your action plan into your life

While designing your action plan, make sure that you can integrate it into your life. Here, set aside sufficient time for you to implement your plan. Thus, if you develop an action plan and don't have the time to devote to implementing it, then you will not implement that plan, and your self-help efforts will eventually founder. This is such an important point that I suggest that you keep it at the forefront of your mind when designing your plan. It is better to restructure your action plan to reflect the time you are prepared to devote to it than try to force yourself to find the time to enable you to carry out your plan.

List problematic situations

Your main adversity theme explains why you find certain situations problematic. However, to deal with the adversity, you need to face the situations which embody the adversity. Consequently, make a comprehensive list of these situations.

Outline the order in which you are going to face the situations

Once you have a made a list of the problematic situations, you first need to exclude any situations that are not relevant for you to face. With the remaining situations, I suggest that you list them in the order in which you choose to face them. It is important that the order makes sense to you. The professional therapy literature suggests that you use the concept of hierarchy to guide your order. This involves you ranking the situations from the easiest to face to the most difficult. My own suggestion is that you choose to face a situation that is challenging for you to face, but not overwhelming. Making this judgement calls upon you to be honest with yourself. For you to change, you need a sense of challenge. Facing an adversity-related situation is difficult and if you think that you can do this easily, then you are not fully facing an adversity. However, you also want to avoid doing something that genuinely seems overwhelming for you at any particular point in time. Otherwise you will become discouraged and may be tempted to abandon self-help altogether. As you progress, you will find that what you previously found overwhelming will become just a challenge for you and, consequently, you will be able to face it. Whichever order you choose, however, it needs to reflect the practicalities of your life and what is most relevant for you.

It is worth remembering that when you face an adversity-related situation, the important point is that you think that the adversity may occur. Whether it does or not is less relevant as the power lies in you practising your solution, having assumed that the adversity will occur.

Construct a timetable for facing the situations

Once you have constructed an order for facing your listed situations, the next stage in developing your action plan is to construct a timetable which will help you to deal with the 'when' of implementation. If you have a timetable, then it will both remind you to take action and serve as a framework to identify if, when and why you have decided *not* to take action. This, of course, is known as procrastination and serves as a major obstacle to implementing your action plan. I will discuss obstacles to implementing your action plan presently.

Once again, I want to emphasise the importance of developing a realistic timetable and one to which you are willing to commit.

List your chosen solution and its variants

You will have long since chosen your solution and made a written note of it. However, when it comes to developing an action plan, I suggest that you write the solution out again and then whenever your plan indicates that you are ready to face an adversity-related situation, make any modifications to the solution based on the situation you are facing. Thus, your solution may point to a way of responding effectively to adversity-related situations in general, whereas when you are facing a specific situation, it is useful to modify the general solution so that it is situation-specific. For example, your general solution might include developing a general flexible and non-extreme attitude towards being criticised, while your specific solution would outline a specific version of that general attitude when you think of being criticised by a specific person in a specific situation.

Incorporate feedback sessions into the action plan

When you come to implementing your action plan, it is important that you learn from your experiences in facing problematic situations while utilising your chosen solution. As such, I recommend that you resolve to have dedicated feedback sessions with yourself after every episode of implementation and that you incorporate these into the timetable that frames your action plan.

Establish signposts for improvement

Another important part of developing an action plan is establishing signposts for improvement. The only real way of gauging the outcome of your chosen solutions is with reference to your nominated problem and problem-related goal. Ask yourself what would tell you that you are making progress in dealing with your problem or moving towards your goal. Taking this tack, you might want to specify what would constitute 25%, 50% and 75% improvement concerning your problem or 25%, 50% and 75% progress towards your goal.

You also might find it helpful to use 'frequency, intensity and duration' criteria in relation to your nominated problem and problem-related goal. Concerning your problem, you are deemed to be making progress if you experience your problem less frequently, with less intensity and with less duration than hitherto. Similarly, concerning your goal, you are deemed to be making progress if you experience your goal with increasing frequency, with greater intensity and with greater duration than hitherto.

List your strengths and incorporate them into your action plan

I mentioned in Chapter 4 that single-session therapists recommend that clients identify their strengths and use them during the session. This also applies when you are working to develop your action plan in self-help therapy. Having listed your strengths, consider how you can use them as you develop your action plan. This will serve as a reminder to use them when you come to implement the plan.

List external resources and incorporate them into your action plan

I also mentioned in Chapter 4 that single-session therapists recommend that clients identify external resources and use them if relevant during the session. Again, this also applies when you develop your action plan in self-help therapy. You may nominate resources provided by people whom you know or by people you may not know who work in helping organisations. It is useful if you specify what kind of help can be provided by which people.

Identify possible obstacles and a way of addressing them

When you come to implement your action plan, you may well encounter obstacles to its implementation. While it is important that you address an obstacle when you encounter it, there is also much merit from identifying possible obstacles in advance and devising ways of dealing with them.

Implement your action plan

An action plan is like a roadmap which offers you an overarching view of what you need to do to address your nominated plan and work towards your problem-related goal (i.e. your solution) and where and when you need to implement the solution. This may best be seen as you taking a general focus. When you implement your solution, you do so one step at a time, and therefore your focus is more specific.

Once you have devised your action plan, you are ready to implement it. This involves you taking the following steps:

1. Be clear with yourself what situation you are going to face. As you do so, focus on the adversity and assume temporarily that it will occur.
2. Develop a situation-specific version of the solution you developed earlier in the process.
3. Specify one or more of your strengths that you might bring into play while putting the solution into practice.
4. Decide if it will help you to use an external resource while putting the solution into practice.
5. If you think it will be helpful, rehearse the solution in your mind's eye before carrying it out in real life. As you do so, keep the situation clearly in mind, particularly focusing on

the adversity that is at the heart of the problem. See your-self putting the solution into practice, but avoid picturing yourself doing so with mastery. See yourself struggling but implementing it anyway.

6. Implement the solution and do so even though you may experience the troublesome emotion that is a feature of your problem. Also, implement the solution even though it is prob-able that you may feel uncomfortable doing so. Change is uncomfortable. Please bear this in mind going forward.

7. Before you go into the adversity-related situation, I suggest that you take some time to get yourself into the right frame of mind to implement your solution.

8. Single-session therapists encourage their clients to reflect on the session they have just had and to take away what they have learned from the session. Similarly, after you have implemented your solution in the adversity-related situation you have faced, I suggest that you go somewhere and reflect on the experience. This involves you identifying any obstacles you encountered during the episode and coming up with a plan to deal with the obstacle before your next solution-implementation episode. It also involves you deciding what you are going to take away from this episode that you can carry forward to the next.

9. Periodically, review your progress and make modifications to any relevant aspect of your action plan as you see fit.

In the next chapter, I will take a closer look at a topic that I have referred to in this and previous chapters – identifying and dealing with obstacles to change. For if you don't deal effectively with these obstacles, you will not sustain the change process and you will not achieve your problem-related goals.

Chapter 13

Identify and deal with obstacles to change

Overview

In this chapter, I will focus on the issue of obstacles to change and the importance of identifying them and responding constructively to them. Dealing with obstacles, in my view, is at the heart of the change process. Whether you do so in advance or after the fact, unless you do so effectively, whatever progress you make towards solving your nominated problem will be short-lived. First, I will detail the most common obstacles to change that you are likely to encounter. These are personal obstacles, interpersonal obstacles and environmental obstacles, and I will discuss how you can respond to them effectively. Second, I will encourage you to develop your own response to the obstacle and then to consider what REBT (the professional framework we are using in this book) has to say on the subject before you decide on which approach to the obstacle you are going to employ. Third, I will distinguish between a lapse and a relapse and show how dealing with the former can help prevent the latter. Finally, I will discuss the issue of vulnerability factors and how to deal with these to enable you to sustain and even enhance your gains.

The nature of obstacles to change

Paraphrasing the words of William Shakespeare, 'the course of true change does not run smooth'. This means that as you implement your action plan and strive towards achieving your problem-related goal, it is very likely that things will not always go smoothly. In this section, I will discuss the types of obstacles to change you are likely to encounter. I will explain: i) personal obstacles, ii) interpersonal obstacles and iii) environmental obstacles.

Personal obstacles to change

The source of personal obstacles to change is, as the phrase makes clear, within you as a person. While I will focus here on personal change obstacles that you can do something about, you will also experience such obstacles that you can't do anything about. With the latter, all you can do is to work around these obstacles as best you can.

Personal obstacles to change that you can do something about

I will first focus on personal obstacles to change that you can do something about. In my view, there are three different categories of such barriers. These are self-esteem related obstacles, discomfort-related obstacles and conflict-related obstacles

Self-esteem related obstacles. This category of obstacles concerns your negative evaluation of yourself and serves to prevent you from using the solution you have selected to achieve your problem-related goal. For example, let's suppose that you have decided to implement a solution that you think will help you deal with criticism more constructively. If you think that you are a failure if you fail to make the solution work, then you won't put this solution into practice. While this will prevent you from thinking you are a failure, it will also prevent you from dealing constructively with criticism by implementing your solution.

Discomfort-related obstacles. This category of obstacles concerns the level of discomfort you are prepared to tolerate and the conditions you think need to be in place before you take action. Generally speaking, these obstacles do not relate to self-esteem issues. For example, if you decide to implement a solution and you become very uncomfortable doing so, then a barrier to change would occur if you choose to stop feeling uncomfortable immediately by stopping implementing the solution. A major discomfort-related obstacle is procrastination. While you may procrastinate to eradicate threats to your self-esteem, the main reason why people tend to procrastinate on implementing their action plan is this: they insist on the presence of certain conditions before they take action (e.g. a sense of control, certainty that their action will be successful, feeling confident, knowing what they are doing). As we will see later in this chapter, the driving force behind procrastination is a person's rigid attitude towards the presence of these favourable conditions.

Conflict-related obstacles. This category of obstacles concerns the conflict that you would feel if you implemented your action plan by executing your solution in an adversity-related situation. For example, if you decide to implement a solution that enables you to deal effectively with being disapproved of by another person, doing so might conflict with your value that it is bad to upset someone by saying 'no' to them. This becomes an obstacle if you resolve your conflict by not implementing the solution. The core of a conflict-related obstacle is that you resolve the conflict by not applying your chosen solution.

Personal obstacles to change that you cannot do anything about

While most of the personal obstacles that you will encounter will be those that you can do something about, some will be those that you can't do anything about. All you can do here is to accept such an obstacle and find a way around it if you can. Personal illness is one such example. If you are ill and house-bound, then there is not much you can do about it apart from trying to get well, but until that happens, you probably will not be able to implement your solution if doing so means leaving your home. You can rehearse the solution in your mind's eye if you are well enough, which may be a good way around the obstacle, but facing the planned adversity-related situation can be legitimately ruled out until things change and you can do something about this barrier.

Interpersonal obstacles to change

The source of interpersonal obstacles to change is, as you might expect, another person or group of people. While I will again focus here on interpersonal change obstacles that you can influence, you will also experience such obstacles that you can't do anything about. With the latter, as before, all you can do is to work around these obstacles as best you can.

Interpersonal obstacles to change that you can do something about

An interpersonal obstacle occurs in the form of something to do with another person which, in reality or in your mind, stops you from implementing your action plan. When you first encounter such an obstacle, you do not know whether or not you can do something about the obstacle. As such, I suggest you assume that you can do something about it until you discover otherwise.

Doing something to address an interpersonal obstacle involves you recognising that you need to change the way you relate to the other person with the intention of eliciting a different response from them, which results in the removal of the obstacle. This may mean changing the way you act towards the other person or the way you talk to them or, of course, both. You may need to experiment with different forms of behaviour and talk before you elicit a productive change or conclude that this interpersonal obstacle is one that you can't do anything about.

Interpersonal obstacles to change that you cannot do anything about

Once you have concluded that you cannot do anything about the interpersonal obstacle to implementing your action plan, then there are two things that you can do. First, you can remove yourself from the person or group of people who constitute the interpersonal obstacle and implement your action plan where these people are not present and thus bypass the obstacle. Second, you need to ask yourself whether there is any way that you can implement your action plan even though the interpersonal obstacle exists. Would a change of attitude towards the interpersonal obstacle render it a non-obstacle? If so, which attitude do you think would help you to do this and what will it take to develop this attitude?

Environmental obstacles to change

Environmental obstacles to change constitute barriers to you implementing your action plan that reside in the non-interpersonal environment. Drawing from what I have already discussed, environmental obstacles can be addressed as follows:

- Change the aspect of the environment that constitutes the obstacle so that the barrier does not exist.
- If you can't change the obstacle, change your attitude towards it, and then bypass it, if possible, so that while the obstacle still exists, you can still implement your action plan, perhaps in modified form.

Dealing effectively with obstacles to change

Let me remind you at this point that by an obstacle to change I mean a barrier that results in you not implementing your chosen solution in an adversity-related situation that you had decided to face. It is one thing to understand what an obstacle is and to which category it belongs; it is another thing to deal with it effectively. I mentioned earlier in the book that it is better to identify and deal with an obstacle *before* it has occurred than it is to deal with it *once* it has occurred. However, the important thing is to respond to the obstacle effectively irrespective of when it occurs.

Single-session therapy, in my view, is best seen as an integration of what the client brings to the process and what the therapist brings to the process. Consequently, in this section, I will discuss your personal response to obstacles, how REBT suggests that you approach the issue and the importance of choosing your own ultimate response based on either of these approaches or an integration of the two.

Choosing your own response to an obstacle to change

While you will wish to approach the issue of choosing your own response to an obstacle to change in your own way – after all, it is *your* approach – I will offer a structure that you might find helpful (see Table 13.1). You may wish to use this table to structure your written notes.

Identify the obstacle

Here you need to discover the nature of the obstacle. What makes the obstacle an obstacle? Is it primarily a personal obstacle, an interpersonal obstacle or an environmental obstacle? State the obstacle in your own words in the appropriate space in Table 13.1. If you struggle with identifying the obstacle, ask yourself what one thing needs to be changed that will enable you to face the adversity-related situation as planned. The factor that you have selected is, in all likelihood, the obstacle that needs to be addressed.

Identify previous attempts to address the obstacle

In single-session therapy (SST), the therapist often encourages the client to identify previous attempts to solve their nominated problem, and I have suggested that you also do this in SST-informed self-help (see Table 11.1). This principle also applies to dealing with your identified obstacle to change. There is a good chance that you have met such an obstacle before and have tried to address it. So, think of those times and list what was helpful about what you did and what was not helpful in the appropriate space in Table 13.1.

Table 13.1 Choosing your own response to an obstacle to change

Obstacle	Helpful and Unhelpful Elements of Previous Attempts to Deal with the Obstacle	Inner Strengths and External Resources that You Can Use to Address the Obstacle	Suggested Responses to Deal with the Obstacle (Select the best response after evaluating them by marking it with an *)	Evaluate the Suggested Responses
	Helpful Elements: Unhelpful Elements:	Inner Strengths: External Resources:	1. 2. 3. 4.	1. 2. 3. 4.

*Identify inner strengths and external resources that you can
use to address the obstacle*

In the same way that you identified inner strengths and external
resources to help you when you formulated your chosen solution
to your nominated problem, you can do likewise when thinking
about designing an effective response to your identified obstacle
to change. There is a space to write these down in Table 13.1.

Brainstorm possible responses to the identified obstacle

Next, I suggest that you brainstorm possible responses to the obstacle that incorporate some of the information noted above. When
you brainstorm, you come up with several solutions spontaneously
without evaluating them until you have completed the task.

Consider your responses and select one

After you have finished brainstorming, stand back and consider
each possible solution and ask yourself i) how effective it is likely
to be in addressing the obstacle effectively and ii) if you can see
yourself implementing it. Go through your list until you have
selected the best available solution.

A professional approach to dealing with obstacles
to change

Before you settle on a response to the obstacle, I suggest that you
first consider what REBT has to offer you in this regard.[1] REBT
has most to offer when the obstacle that you have come across
is in the form of an emotionally problematic response to something. In these circumstances, REBT recommends the use of an
ABC framework as presented in Table 13.2.

REBT suggests that you use the framework in the following
way, although you might find a different order suits you better.
You might find completing Table 13.3 helpful to you.

---

1 I am discussing REBT in this book because it is the approach that I bring to the
work. There are, of course, other professional approaches available for you to
draw from.

Table 13.2 REBT's ABC framework

Situation	
Adversity ('A')	
Basic Attitudes ('B') **(Rigid and extreme)**	**Basic Attitudes ('B')** **(Flexible and non-extreme)**
Rigid Attitude =	Flexible Attitude =
Awfulising Attitude =	Non-awfulising Attitude =
Discomfort Intolerance Attitude =	Discomfort Tolerance Attitude =
Devaluation Attitude =	Unconditional Acceptance Attitude =
Consequences ('C') **(Unhealthy and dysfunctional)**	**Consequences ('C')** **(Healthy and functional)**
Emotional =	Emotional =
Behavioural =	Behavioural =
Thinking =	Thinking =

These serve as potential adversity-related goals for the client.

Table 13.3 Using REBT to deal with an obstacle to change

Obstacle	
'C' (Emotions, Behaviours Thoughts)	
'A' (Adversity)	
'B' (Basic Attitudes)	Rigid Attitude: Flexible Attitude:
	Awfulising Attitude: Non-awfulising Attitude:
	Discomfort Intolerance Attitude: Discomfort Tolerance Attitude:
	Devaluation Attitude: Unconditional Acceptance Attitude:

Identify the obstacle

The first step is for you to specify and describe the obstacle, as you did when adopting your own approach to dealing with the obstacle (see above), and write this in the relevant space in Table 13.3. Remember that the obstacle explains why you did not implement your action plan in a given situation

Identify your responses to the situation in which the obstacle occurred

Here, you need to identify the most troublesome emotion that you experienced in the context of the obstacle and what you did and thought when you experienced the troublesome emotion. These emotions, behaviours and thoughts constitute the consequences of 'B' (which I will discuss presently) and, as such, go in the section in Table 13.3 marked 'C'.

Identify the obstacle-related adversity

The next step is to find out what you were most disturbed about in the situation where you experienced the obstacle. This is 'A' or adversity. In the same way that at the heart of your nominated problem lies an adversity that you find problematic, at the heart of your obstacle lies another adversity, which may be the same as in your nominated problem or it might be different. If you find it difficult to identify the obstacle-related adversity, you can do one of two things. First, use the troublesome emotion at 'C' (e.g. anxiety) to ask yourself a question like: 'What did I find most anxiety-provoking in the situation that led me to abandon the use of my solution?' Second, ask yourself the question: 'If I could have had one ingredient that would have meant that I would not have experienced the troublesome emotion, what would that have been?' The opposite of this ingredient is often the obstacle-related adversity. When you have identified the adversity, write it in the space in Table 13.3 under 'A'.

Discover your attitude

REBT is based on the ABC model of human responsiveness that I outlined in Table 13.2. I suggest that you have this table in front of you when taking this step, which is to discover what basic attitude you held at 'B' towards the adversity at 'A' which led you to experience the troublesome emotion and to abandon your action plan at 'C'. To reiterate, REBT's view is that the presence of an adversity does not create an obstacle to change. Rather, it is your basic attitude towards the adversity that accounts for the obstacle. Therefore, if you change your attitude towards the adversity, you change your emotion and your behaviour towards it, which means that the presence of the adversity no longer constitutes an obstacle to change.

Table 13.2 outlines the attitudes that you hold towards the obstacle-related adversity that explains why you did not implement your action plan, and it also outlines the attitudes that you need to adopt to implement it even if the adversity remains.[2]

As you answer the following questions, please be aware that REBT argues that you hold at least one of the four attitudes to be presented. Do not assume, however, that you have to hold all four.

Was my attitude towards the adversity rigid or flexible? For example, we know that you would prefer this adversity did not exist, but were you demanding that it must not exist (rigid) or not (flexible)?

Was my attitude towards the adversity one of badness with horror (extreme) or badness without horror (non-extreme)? For example, we know that you think that it is bad that the adversity occurred, but do you think that it is awful that it happened or do you think that it isn't awful that it happened?

Was my attitude towards the adversity one of intolerance (extreme) or tolerance (non-extreme) of the discomfort I experienced when facing the adversity? For example, we know that you think that it is a struggle for you to tolerate the discomfort

2 Remember that in REBT we proceed on the idea that the adversity actually exists or that you deem it to exist.

involved in facing the adversity, but do you think that you can't tolerate this discomfort or do you think that you can tolerate it and it is worth it to you to do so?

Was my attitude towards the adversity one of devaluation of self/other/life (extreme) or unconditional acceptance of self/ other/life (non-extreme)? For example, we know that you think that the adversity is bad, but do you hold an attitude of devaluation of self/other/life or an attitude of unconditional acceptance of self/other/life. The target of your devaluation attitude or unconditional acceptance attitude depends on who you hold responsible for the adversity.

Choose your attitude and support your choice

In answering the questions posed above, you have probably indicated that your attitude towards the obstacle-related adversity is rigid and/or extreme. REBT argues that there is a flexible alternative to your rigid attitude and a non-extreme alternative to your extreme attitude. I included these alternatives in the questions that I suggested that you asked yourself about the attitudes that you hold about the obstacle-related adversity. The next step is for you to take the alternative(s) to the rigid and/or extreme attitudes you identified and really imagine yourself holding these alternative attitudes while facing the obstacle-related adversity. Get into the flexible and/or non-extreme mindset. If you do this, then you will probably notice that your feelings change towards the adversity, which no longer appears the obstacle that it seemed to you when your mindset was rigid and/or extreme. So, you need to ask yourself which attitude you want to adopt going forward and when you have made your choice, support it by giving yourself reasons for it. What might help here is for you to imagine teaching a group of children the value of the flexible and non-extreme mindsets over the rigid and extreme mindsets responsible for the adversity becoming an obstacle.

Act in ways that are consistent with your chosen attitudes

Once you have made your choice of attitude concerning dealing with the obstacle, then you need to act in ways that are consistent with it. This usually means facing the obstacle-related adversity while keeping your chosen attitude in mind as you do so. In this way, you will be able to deal with this and any related obstacles that you might encounter. As you go forward making your behaviour consistent with your chosen attitude, as far as you can, guard against using any behaviours or ways of thinking that are designed to keep you safe but will result in taking your focus away from this adversity. Refraining from doing this is important, but you may feel strong levels of discomfort, at least initially. If you do so, please accept and tolerate this discomfort. It won't last for long and tolerating it will help you overcome your obstacle to change.

Designing and implementing your ultimate response to an obstacle to change

You have now considered both your own response to the obstacle to you implementing your action plan and what REBT has to offer on the same issue. At this point, you can go forward with your own response, REBT's suggested response or an integrated response where you take what you consider to be the best from each of the aforementioned approaches to form what I call your ultimate response to the obstacle to change. Once you have done this, implement it while considering the points I have made above concerning facing your obstacle-related adversity.

Responding to lapses and relapse and dealing with vulnerability factors

There are several other issues that I want to cover before bringing this discussion of dealing with obstacles to change to a close.

Lapses and how to deal with them

In my view, a lapse is a minor return to your problem. It is far from an unusual occurrence, and therefore my advice to you is to accept it when it happens, but do not like it. This will help you to review what happened that led you to return to the problem state and to identify the key factor or factors responsible for this. Once you have done this, draw up a plan to deal with these factors if you encounter them again.

You might also find it useful to do the following:

- Ask someone to support you when you lapse and to help you learn from the experience.
- Use your strengths in responding to a lapse.
- Identify and use past successful experience in dealing with lapses in both the problem area and in other areas.

Preventing relapse

In my view, a relapse is a full return to your problem. Some people refer to it as 'going back to square one' concerning their problem. Relapse is more likely to occur when you have not dealt productively with lapses or you respond to a lapse by giving up your self-help project. The latter situation comes about if you hold a rigid attitude towards a lapse. Thus, if your attitude towards a lapse is 'It must not occur' and it does, you are more likely to stop helping yourself than you would be if you held a flexible attitude towards a lapse (e.g. 'I don't want to experience a lapse, but that does not mean that it must not happen'). So, if you want to prevent relapse, then develop a flexible attitude towards lapses and deal with them effectively if and when they occur.

Dealing with vulnerability factors. Another important part of preventing relapse involves you identifying what are often referred to as 'vulnerability factors'. These are factors whose presence provides the context i) where you would not routinely deal with your problem, and ii) where you would, unwittingly in fact, maintain the problem. It is important that you identify and deal with these factors. You may have to avoid them initially until you have had some success at implementing your action plan. However, sooner or later you need to face these factors and deal with them so that they are no longer 'vulnerability' factors. Using the 'challenging, but not overwhelming' rule of thumb that I discussed earlier in this chapter may help you in this respect.

Examples of vulnerability factors are: i) situations where it is very easy for you to revert to your problem; ii) people who make it very difficult for you to implement your action plan or who discourage you from doing so; iii) your philosophy of short-range hedonism which leads you to prioritise pleasure over self-help.

Responding to relapse

Sometimes in a self-change programme, for whatever reason, you may relapse. How you deal with this is crucial to what you do next in your self-therapy. From the above discussion you will see that there are three possible responses: your own, that suggested by REBT and an integration of these first two responses.

In designing your own response to relapse, stand back and ask yourself how you would encourage others to respond to relapse, as well as how you would hope a compassionate response would encourage you to respond to it. These two scenarios will suggest your own response to relapse, the purpose of which is for you to learn from the experience and renew your commitment to self-change rather than giving up on it.

REBT's approach to relapse response encourages you to accept that sometimes relapse occurs. It argues that while this is most unfortunate, it does not constitute an 'end of the world' experience. If you adopt this attitude, then you will be able to stand back and undertake a rigorous analysis of the factors that accounted for your relapse. This review will be enhanced if you take responsibility for your relapse without devaluing yourself for it. In sum, REBT recommends that you adopt a mindset towards relapse based on the attitudes of flexibility, anti-awfulising and unconditional self-acceptance.

As argued above, your ultimate response to relapse could be your own, REBT's or an amalgam of the two.

In the next chapter, I will discuss how you can maintain your gains once you have made them, and how to generalise your learning from dealing with your nominated problem to other problems you may have.

Chapter 14

Maintain your gains and generalise your learning

Overview

In this chapter, I argue that you need to commit yourself to using your solution regularly if you want to maintain your self-help gains. Then, I will consider what you need to do to maintain the gains that you have made from helping yourself and also how you can generalise these gains. In this respect, I will first discuss how you can apply your solution to different situations where the same problem-related adversity features and to different, but related adversities. Then, I will discuss how you can take the skills you have learned when dealing with your first nominated problem and apply these to different problems. Finally, I will show you how you can take the healthy attitudes that REBT considers to be the foundations of constructive responses to life's adversities and apply these across the board.

Maintain your gains

As anybody who has succeeded at losing weight and at hitting their target in this area will tell you, this is not the end of the story. Indeed, some would say that the real work of change begins at this point. When you have reached a goal, there is an initial level of excitement, followed by a sense of satisfaction, and if you are not careful, there may follow a feeling of complacency. You have worked hard to achieve your goal, and you consider that you deserve a rest. So, you relax the reins, and before too long you have reverted to old problem-related habits, and while you may not be back to 'square one', you have slipped back to experiencing your problem again in some shape or form. As I discussed in the previous chapter, if you do not take steps to remedy the situation at this point, then you may experience your problem as you did before you decided to help yourself in the first place. Please review the material in that chapter if this has happened to you.

However, the best way to avoid 'slipping back' to old, but familiar 'problem' ways is to make a definite commitment to maintain the gains you have made through self-help therapy.

Commit yourself to using your problem-related solution regularly

I mentioned above that when you achieve your problem-related goal, it is likely that you will be excited and then experience a sense of satisfaction. There is nothing at all problematic about this and in fact it would be strange if you didn't experience such reactions since you have achieved something that is meaningful to you. The difficulty lies in the complacency that may set in, coupled with the 'relaxing of the reins' and you beginning to stop doing what you did to achieve the goal in the first place. Effectively this means that you have stopped facing adversity while using the solution you developed to deal effectively with that adversity.

Here is an example of what I mean. Jonathan had a problem with not being listened to in conversations, which he responded to with sulkiness and getting angry. In his 'one-at-a-time' self-help sessions, he understood that, in his words, this made him feel like a nothing. His goal was to feel annoyed without being sulkily angry if another person did not listen to him, and his solution to enable him to achieve this goal was the attitude that he was still a somebody in the face of not being listened to and the behaviour of asserting himself if this happened. He practised this solution regularly until he had reached his goal.

Instead of becoming complacent, Jonathan decided that once a week he would seek out a person whose habit was not to listen to him so that he could practise his solution in the face of adversity. He rehearsed this solution in his mind's eye to prepare himself to implement the solution in the real situation. Then he entered the situation and implemented the solution if the adversity materialised in the situation.

As I explained earlier in the book, the importance of mental rehearsal is to help you practise your solution so that you benefit from such practice even when the adversity does not happen in the situation. There are, in fact, two benefits to you if the adversity does happen. First, you are prepared to deal with it from the mental rehearsal you have done. Second, you practised the solution twice in the face of adversity – through mental rehearsal and in the actual situation.

After every practice session, spend some time reflecting on what you learned and digest this learning, in particular by considering how you can apply the solution in other situations and problem areas (to be discussed shortly). This reflection and digestion may lead you to consider refinements to your solution. If so, you should consider how you can incorporate these refinements the next time you plan to practise your solution.

Generalise your gains and what you have learned about emotional problem-solving

So far in this book I have concentrated on helping you to identify and deal with what I have called your nominated problem. This is the problem to which you have chosen to give priority with respect to self-help. Once you have achieved your goal with respect to your nominated problem, you are ready to generalise your gains and your learning. You can do this in different ways.

Same adversity, different situations

If your problem is situation-specific, then you can generalise your gains by dealing with your problem-related adversity in other situations. Many years ago, I helped one of my clients deal with his fear of being criticised by his boss. A few sessions later, he wanted to address his fear of being criticised by his wife. I asked him if he applied what he learned from addressing his fear of his boss's criticism to his fear of his wife's criticism. I remember his reply to this day: 'No. Was I supposed to?' This taught me that people do not automatically generalise their learning and gains from one situation to another and that they have to be reminded and encouraged to do so. So please do not assume that you will naturally be able to deal with other situations where your adversity is likely to feature. You need to work to bring about such generalisation. You can do this by using your chosen solution, modifying it according to the new situations that feature the adversity, and rehearsing its use in your mind's eye before implementing it in the situations themselves.

Different, but related adversities

Another way of generalising your gains is to consider if your solution, duly amended, can be applied to related adversities that may feature in other problems that you may have. If so, then you can make those amendments and develop an action plan you can use in these situations where the new adversity is deemed to feature. Thus, once you are ready to move on from dealing with your problematic response to your problem-related adversity, you can do the following:

- Ask yourself whether you have a problem with similar adversities and, if so, what are they? Thus, Jonathan, who had a problem when people did not listen to him, asked himself whether he also had a problem when, for example, people criticised him, rejected him or treated him unfairly, etc.?
- If so, set goals for dealing with these new problems. Ask yourself what would be a constructive way of dealing with these related adversities?
- Ask yourself whether you can apply the solution that you developed to your original nominated problem to these new problems? The solution may not be exactly the same, but can it be modified to become a constructive solution to these new problems? If so, then develop an action plan you can implement in relevant adversity-related situations.

Different problems, same skills

In addition to dealing with your nominated problem and generalising your gains to related adversities, you may have other problems which are very different from your nominated problem and those related problems may feature similar adversities to the one at the core of your nominated problem. If so, you can generalise your learning by using as many of the relevant skills that you used to deal with your nominated problem as you can to deal with your different problem(s). In doing so, don't forget you can use your own responses and those suggested by REBT (the professional framework that I am applying in this book).

• Describe your problem and the situations in which it occurs.
• Identify the main troublesome emotion that features in this problem and its associated behaviour and thinking.
• Identify the main adversity theme that features in the problem.
• Identify your attitudes towards the adversity theme that contribute to the problem.
• Set a goal with respect to the problem.
• List the previous attempts you made to deal with the problem. Note any helpful features in these attempts that you could use in developing your solution and those unhelpful features that you need to cast aside.
• Identify any internal strengths and external resources that you can use in addressing the problem.
• Brainstorm possible solutions to the problem and then evaluate them.
• Select the solution that seems the most likely to help you to achieve your problem-related goal and the one that you can best integrate into your life.
• Rehearse that solution before deciding to implement it.
• Devise an action plan to implement the solution.
• Anticipate and problem-solve potential obstacles to carrying out the situation.
• Implement the solution.
• Maintain the solution.

Use flexible and non-extreme attitudes across the board

The final approach to generalising your gains is derived from REBT. In Chapter 11, I discussed REBT's view that a healthy way to deal with problem-related adversities is to develop a set of flexible and non-extreme attitudes towards these adversities (see Table 14.1). You can then use one or more of these healthy attitudes to deal with whatever adversity you may encounter in life. Let me detail how you can do this. First, you need to select which one or two healthy attitudes will best help you to face whatever adversity you encounter. Second, you need to apply this attitude when needed, as shown below.

Table 14.1 Solutions to dealing with adversities: healthy attitudes

Flexible Attitude	The idea that you would prefer it if the adversity did not occur without demanding that it must be that way
Non-awfulising Attitude	The idea that while it is bad if the adversity occurs, it is not the end of the world if it does so
Discomfort Tolerance Attitude	The idea that while it is a struggle for you to tolerate it if the adversity occurred, you can tolerate it if it did, it is worth doing so, you are willing to do so and you are going to do so
Unconditional Acceptance Attitude	The idea that while the adversity is bad, you are a fallible human being (if you are deemed responsible for the adversity), the other person is fallible (if the other person is deemed responsible for the adversity) and life is a complex mixture of good, bad and neutral aspects (if life is deemed responsible for the adversity)

Use a flexible attitude across the board

Below I show how you can generalise your gains by adopting a flexible attitude towards whichever adversity you face. While I will suggest a form of words, please free to use whatever language suits you.

Suggested Form of Words	Example
'My preference is that the *adversity* did not happen,[1] but it doesn't have to be the way I want it to be.'	'My preference is that my boss does not *criticise* me, but it does not have to be the way I want it to be.'

You can use this flexible attitude before, during and after facing an adversity. Thus, taking the above example, you can use the flexible attitude before meeting your boss (who may criticise you) and after the meeting if your boss did criticise you. You can even also use an abbreviated version of the flexible attitude while your boss is criticising you.

Use a non-awfulising attitude across the board

This is how you can generalise your gains by adopting a non-awfulising attitude again towards whichever adversity you face. As before, while I will suggest a form of words, please free to use whatever language suits you.

Suggested Form of Words	Example
' It is bad if the *adversity* happened.[2] but it would not be the end of the world.'	'It would be bad if my boss criticises me, but it would not be the end of the world.'

1 Feel free to use whichever tense of verb makes most sense (past, present or future).
2 As before, feel free to use whichever tense of verb makes most sense (past, present or future).

As with a flexible attitude, you can use this non-awfulising attitude before, during and after facing an adversity. Thus, again taking the above example, you can use the non-awfulising attitude before meeting your boss and afterwards, if your boss did criticise you. As suggested before, you can even also use an abbreviated version of the non-awfulising attitude while the person is criticising you.

Use a discomfort tolerance attitude across the board

By now, you will be familiar with the idea of taking a healthy attitude and applying it across the board whenever you encounter an adversity. This is how you can generalise your gains by adopting a discomfort tolerance attitude towards whichever adversity you face. As before, while I will suggest a form of words, please free to use whatever language suits you.

Suggested Form of Words	Example
'It is a struggle tolerating the discomfort that I would feel if the *adversity* happened,[3] but I could tolerate it, it is worth tolerating, I am willing to tolerate it, and I am going to do so.'	'It would be a struggle tolerating the discomfort that I would feel if my boss criticised me, but I could tolerate it, it is worth tolerating, I am willing to tolerate it, and I am going to do so.'

As with the other healthy attitudes I have discussed, you can use this discomfort tolerance attitude before, during and after facing an adversity. Thus, again taking the above example, you can use the discomfort tolerance attitude before meeting your boss and afterwards, if they did criticise you. You can, as suggested before, even also use an abbreviated version of the discomfort tolerance attitude while the person is criticising you.

---

3 As before, feel free to use whichever tense of verb makes most sense (past, present or future).

Use an unconditional acceptance attitude across the board

Finally, here is how you can generalise your gains by adopting an unconditional acceptance attitude towards whichever adversity you face. As before, I will suggest a form of words. However, use whatever language suits you best.

Suggested Form of Words	Example
'While the adversity is bad,[4] I am a fallible human being (if I deem myself as responsible for the adversity), the other person is fallible (if I deem the other person responsible for the adversity) and life is a complex mixture of good, bad and neutral aspects (if I deem life responsible for the adversity).'	'While it would be bad if my boss criticised me, it would not prove that I have any less value as a person. I am still a fallible human being whether or not my boss criticises me.'

As you now know, you can use this unconditional acceptance attitude before, during and after facing an adversity. Thus, again taking the above example, you can use the unconditional self-acceptance attitude (in this case) before meeting your boss and afterwards, if they did criticise you. You can, as suggested before, even also use an abbreviated version of the unconditional self-acceptance attitude while the person is criticising you.

We have now come to the end of the book. I hope that you have found it useful. I would welcome any feedback you have for me about how I can improve the book in any future edition(s). Please send it to me at windy@windydryden.com

---

4 As before, feel free to use whichever tense of verb makes most sense (past, present or future).

Index